Explosive
HOCKEY
TRIVIA

GREYSTONE BOOKS
Douglas & McIntyre Publishing Group
Vancouver/Toronto/New York

For Edgar Andrew Collard.—Don Weekes

Copyright © 2001 by Don Weekes
01 02 03 04 05   5 4 3 2 1

Greystone Books
A division of Douglas & McIntyre Ltd.
2323 Quebec Street, Suite 201
Vancouver, British Columbia V5T 4S7
www.greystonebooks.ca

CANADIAN CATALOGUING IN PUBLICATION DATA
Weekes, Don.
    Explosive hockey trivia

    ISBN 1-55054-851-4

    1. Hockey—Miscellanea. 2. National Hockey League—Miscellanea.
I. Title.
GV847.W3618 2001   796.962'64   C2001-910481-2

Editing by Brian Scrivener
Typeset by Tanya Lloyd / Spotlight Designs
Cover design by Peter Cocking
Cover photograph by John Russell/Bruce Bennett Studios
Printed and bound in Canada by Friesens

We gratefully acknowledge the financial support of the Canada Council for the Arts, the British Columbia Ministry of Tourism, Small Business and Culture, and the Government of Canada through the Book Publishing Industry Development Program (BPIDP) for its publishing activities.

Don Weekes *is a television producer and writer with CFCF 12 in Montreal. This is his seventeenth hockey trivia book.*

CONTENTS

PREFACE

Until Scott Stevens won the Conn Smythe Trophy in 2000 as playoff MVP, he had never won a major individual trophy in 18 NHL seasons. This despite the fact that the New Jersey captain remained among the league's top defenseman for almost two decades, was named to the NHL's All-Rookie Team in 1983 and twice chosen a First All-Star. Stevens, one of those defensive stalwarts often underrated, has also twice been voted runner-up in Norris Trophy balloting as top blueliner.

When he was finally honoured by the hockey establishment, Stevens won big, scoring hockey's "other" most important MVP award, the Smythe, and his second Stanley Cup. His leadership and fearless play set the physical tone of each playoff series in 2000.

In Round 1, against Florida, Stevens scored the first goal of the series, scored the winner in the second game and shut down the speedy Pavel Bure, as the Devils swept the Panthers in four straight. In Round 2, his toughness finished off the Leafs in six games. Toronto's Mats Sundin accused Stevens of playing "borderline" dirty.

In Round 3, against the Flyers, he kept big John LeClair from scoring a single goal, knocked heavyweight Eric Lindros out of the playoffs with a punishing open-ice hit (that will be talked about for years) and spear-headed New Jersey to an amazing comeback after being down 3–1 in the series. In the finals, Stevens's work ethic and power simply ground down the Dallas Stars and led the Devils to their second Stanley Cup in six seasons with a 4–2 series win. Afterwards, he admitted to raising the Stanley Cup with some pain, an affliction from a pinched nerve in his shoulder that he had kept hidden for three playoff rounds.

In our 17th hockey trivia book, we celebrate the Scott Stevens of the hockey world—those explosive champions who so often go unrecognized in our game. Enjoy.

DON WEEKES
February 4, 2001

1
CRACKING THE LINE-UP

In December 2000 *Sports Illustrated* polled athletes from North America's four major team sports to pick their game's loudest fans, best groupies and most loyal spectators. In hockey, the Flyers had the toughest and scariest followers; the Red Wings were cheered on by the league's loudest supporters and the Hurricanes and Lightning by the stupidest ticket holders; the Kings were pursued by the best groupies; and the most knowledgeable and most devoted fans resided at the Air Canada Centre in Toronto.

In our first chapter we test your level of hockey fanaticism with a series of general questions to get you into our starting line-up. Don't forget, it's not necessarily how much you know, but how you play the game. Trust your instincts.

(Solutions are on page 7)

(Solutions are on page 7)

1.1 **Which NHL team has earned the best record in season openers?**
A. The New Jersey Devils
B. The St. Louis Blues
C. The Colorado Avalanche
D. The Montreal Canadiens

1.2 **Who is the youngest team captain in NHL history?**
A. Edmonton's Wayne Gretzky
B. Detroit's Steve Yzerman
C. Colorado/Quebec's Joe Sakic
D. Tampa Bay's Vincent Lecavalier

1.3 Prior to Chris Pronger winning the Hart Trophy as league MVP in 2000, when was the last time a defenseman captured the coveted award?
A. Ray Bourque–1987
B. Rod Langway–1984
C. Denis Potvin–1976
D. Bobby Orr–1972

1.4 Who was credited with scoring a goal during a game in 2000–01, although he never actually put the puck in the net?
A. Marian Hossa of the Ottawa Senators
B. Trent Klatt of the Vancouver Canucks
C. Todd Marchant of the Edmonton Oilers
D. Darcy Tucker of the Toronto Maple Leafs

1.5 Who is "Mad Mike"?
A. Mike Modano
B. Mike Keenan
C. Mike Milbury
D. Mike Richter

1.6 According to a 2000 poll in *The Hockey News* which season is considered No. 1 in NHL history?
A. Maurice Richard's 50-goal season in 1944–45
B. Bobby Orr's 120-point season in 1969–70
C. Wayne Gretzky's 212-point season in 1981–82
D. Mario Lemieux's 199-point season in 1988–89

1.7 The term "Golden Helmet" is common in many European hockey leagues. Who wears the "Golden Helmet"?
A. The highest scorer on a team
B. The highest-paid player in the league
C. The player with the most points in the league
D. The player with the fewest penalty minutes in the league

1.8 As of 1999–2000 the six Sutter brothers—Brian, Darryl, Duane, Brent, Rich and Ron—had played a total of 4,973 NHL games. What were their combined totals?
A. 1,019 goals, 2,931 points and 5,212 penalty minutes
B. 1,319 goals, 2,931 points and 5,212 penalty minutes
C. 1,319 goals, 2,931 points and 7,212 penalty minutes
D. 1,619 goals, 2,931 points and 7,212 penalty minutes

1.9 What was the highest draft position of a player (who didn't sign with his original club) who re-entered the draft?
A. First overall
B. Fifth overall
C. Ninth overall
D. 19th overall

1.10 What special feature was included in some trading card packs of the Be A Player 2000/2001 Memorabilia Series?
A. Official NHL bubble gum
B. Holographic player pictures
C. Genuine player autographs
D. Swatches of actual equipment fabric

1.11 In their first game against their former captain Mark Messier, the Vancouver Canucks played to what result against the New York Rangers?
A. Vancouver won 4–3
B. Vancouver lost 4–3
C. Vancouver tied 4–4
D. Vancouver earned a regulation tie, losing 4–3 in overtime

1.12 What NHL club alternated team captains every month in 2000–01?
A. The Nashville Predators
B. The San Jose Sharks
C. The Florida Panthers
D. The Minnesota Wild

1.13 Where was Maurice Richard's funeral held in May 2000?
A. At the Molson Centre in downtown Montreal
B. At the Maurice Richard Arena in north-end Montreal
C. At Notre Dame Basilica in Old Montreal
D. On the site of the old Montreal Forum in west-end Montreal

1.14 What Edmonton Oiler in 2000–01 became the first NHLer in league history to score all three goals in a 3–0 game, twice?
A. Ryan Smyth
B. Doug Weight
C. Bill Guerin
D. Todd Marchant

1.15 What is the most number of black players iced by one NHL team?
A. Two players
B. Three players
C. Four players
D. Five players

1.16 After Wayne Gretzky who is the next most accomplished NHLer to come from Brantford, Ontario?
A. Brendan Shanahan
B. Doug Jarvis
C. Doug Gilmour
D. Wendel Clark

1.17 As of 2000–01, how many times has defenseman Scott Stevens been a minus in plus-minus ratings during his 19-year career?

A. Never
B. Only once
C. Three times
D. Five times

1.18 What is considered the top winning percentage attainable by faceoff specialists in the NHL?

A. Between 50 and 60 per cent
B. Between 60 and 70 per cent
C. Between 70 and 80 per cent
D. Between 80 and 90 per cent

1.19 Which NHL coach and former NHLer owns the dubious distinction of playing the most league games from the start of a career without scoring a goal?

A. Larry Robinson
B. Pat Quinn
C. Joel Quenneville
D. Terry Murray

1.20 Which old-time defenseman is considered the first skater to replace an injured goalie for an entire NHL game?

A. Harry Mummery
B. Eddie Shore
C. Sprague Cleghorn
D. Eddie Gerard

1.21 On January 14, 1922, Montreal Canadiens Sprague and Odie Cleghorn each scored four goals in the same game. When was the next time in NHL history teammates each recorded a four-goal night together?

A. 1940–41
B. 1960–61
C. 1980–81
D. 2000–01

1.22 In 1999–2000, the first NHL regular season of four-on-four hockey in five-minute overtime, how many of the 261 overtime periods produced a winning goal?

A. 95 of 261 OT periods
B. 115 of 261 OT periods
C. 135 of 261 OT periods
D. 155 of 261 OT periods

1.23 Which American state has produced the most NHLers?

A. New York
B. Michigan
C. Massachusetts
D. Minnesota

1.24 Which Canadian city has produced the most NHLers?

A. Montreal
B. Toronto
C. Winnipeg
D. Edmonton

CRACKING THE LINE-UP
Answers

1.1   **C. The Colorado Avalanche**

As of 2000–01, the best mark for season-opening games belongs to the Avalanche with a 13–4–5 record after 22 openers. But credit the old Quebec Nordiques for much of the Avs' success here. Since moving to Colorado from Quebec in 1995, the Avs have only scored one opening night victory, on October 6, 1995, a 3–2 win over Detroit. The remaining 12 wins are courtesy of the Nordiques.

BEST TEAM RECORDS IN NHL SEASON OPENERS

Team	GP	W	L	T	Pct.
Colorado	22	13	4	5	.705
New Jersey	27	15	6	6	.667
Montreal	84	44	25	15	.613
Ottawa	9	3	1	5	.611
St. Louis	34	18	11	5	.603

Current to 2000–01

1.2   **D. Tampa Bay's Vincent Lecavalier**

Former coach Jacques Demers knows something about spotting potential captains in young players. After all, it was Demers who handed the Detroit captaincy to Steve Yzerman at just 21 years old in 1986–87. Demers saw the same promise in Lecavalier in Tampa Bay but resisted after Lightning captain Rob Zamuner left at the end of 1998–99. As Demers said, "...it would have been a distraction and he didn't need that at the time." But when captain Chris Gratton was traded in late 1999–2000, the emerging team leader proved to be Lecavalier, who at 20 years became the NHL's youngest-ever player to wear the "C."

1.3   D. Bobby Orr–1972

Prior to Chris Pronger's award in 2000, no defenseman has been named Hart Trophy winner since Bobby Orr won MVP status in three consecutive years (1970, 1971 and 1972). In fact, the 28-year wait has witnessed only four runner-up finishes by blueliners in MVP voting, including Denis Potvin (second to Bobby Clarke in 1976), Rod Langway (second to Wayne Gretzky in 1984), and Ray Bourque twice (second to Wayne Gretzky in 1987 and to Mark Messier in 1990). "I guess I have some pretty big standards to live up to," Pronger said, upon receiving the Hart. Pronger, only the eighth defenseman to capture the MVP trophy in NHL history, follows Orr, Babe Pratt (1944), Tom Anderson (1941), Ebbie Goodfellow (1940), Eddie Shore (1933, 1935, 1936, 1938), Babe Siebert (1937) and Herb Gardiner (1927). Unlike today, when so few defensemen are honoured, between 1933 and 1944 D-men won the Hart an unprecedented eight times.

1.4   B. Trent Klatt of the Vancouver Canucks

It was the phantom goal of 2000–01. The oddity occurred in the last minute of a game at Vancouver's General Motors Place on December 4, 2000. The Canucks were leading the Nashville Predators 5–3 with about a minute left to play, when Nashville's coach, Barry Trotz, pulled goalie Mike Dunham for an extra attacker. Moments later, Canucks winger Trent Klatt broke free with the puck and was about to slide it into the empty net when he was grabbed from behind by Predators defenseman Bubba Berenzweig. Because of the infraction, Klatt was awarded a penalty shot. But rather then have him take the shot at the empty net, the on-ice officials simply awarded him a goal. Afterwards Klatt said, "Was that the ugliest goal of the year or what? I don't remember seeing anything like that before. I don't think I've ever scored without putting the puck in the net."

1.5　C.　Mike Milbury

Calling himself "Mad Mike," Milbury sliced and diced his Islanders roster into an almost unrecognizable team in just a few short years. Some league general managers publicly questioned his deals and as one hockey writer said, "Milbury... makes George Steinbrenner look like the picture of restraint." Although he was working under some financial restraints, the Isles lost perennial 40-goal man Ziggy Palffy; Roberto Luongo, the promising Quebec goaltender; and his entire defensive corps of Bryan Berard, Wade Redden, Darius Kasparaitis, Bryan McCabe and Eric Brewer. Others complained that Milbury ruined the confidence of young players and chased away several rising stars. Mad Mike's report card, after five seasons of shuffling bodies, rates his 2000–01 team as non-improved despite all the deal making.

1.6　B.　Bobby Orr's 120-point season in 1969–70

In "Century of Hockey," *The Hockey News* polled 20 hockey experts and chose Orr's 1969–70 season as the best in league history—ahead of Wayne Gretzky's record 212-point season in 1981–82. During 1969–70 Orr scored 33 goals and 120 points to become the first defenseman in history to win the Art Ross Trophy as scoring champion. He also won every important individual award available, including the Hart Trophy as league MVP, James Norris Trophy as best defenseman and in the playoffs the Stanley Cup and Conn Smythe Trophy as post-season MVP. In a Canadian Press report Orr said: "People say to me: 'How'd you put up numbers like that?' I was blessed with an ability to play the game and to skate. But I was always allowed to play my style, whereas what is happening in the game today is we're not letting players create. It starts long before the pros. It starts with kids. They (coaches) want to teach the trap. If you have a young defenseman who can skate, they want him to throw the puck up along the glass. They don't want him to skate past centre ice. That's really hurting us. It's not fun for the kids. We're not letting them create."

1.7   A.   **The highest scorer on a team**
In several European hockey leagues it is customary for the player who is leading his team in scoring to wear a golden helmet. The practice is similar to what occurs in the Tour de France bicycle race where the overall leader wears a yellow jersey.

1.8   C.   **1,319 goals, 2,931 points and 7,212 penalty minutes**
From 1976–77 when the first Sutter brother, Brian, joined the NHL, until only Ron, the last sibling, remained in 2000–2001, the six Sutters from Viking, Alberta, played in about 5,000 games (more than any other family in NHL history) spanning 24 years. Character players born of prairie grit and brawn, each brother except Darryl recorded careers of more than 1,000 penalty minutes; Brent earned the best offensive numbers, 363 goals and 829 points and played in the most games, 1,111. As of 2000–01, Ron signed with Calgary after being cut by his brother, San Jose coach Darryl Sutter, at the end of 1999–2000.

THE SUTTER FAMILY SAGA

Brother	Teams	Games	Goals	Assist	Pts	PIM
Brian	St.L	779	303	333	636	1,786
Brent	NYI, Chi	1,111	363	466	829	1,054
Darryl	Chi	406	161	118	279	288
Duane	NYI, Chi	731	139	203	342	1,333
Rich	(Six teams)	874	149	166	315	1,411
Ron	(Seven teams)	1,072	204	326	530	1,340
Totals		4,973	1,319	1,612	2,931	7,212

Current to 1999-2000

1.9   C.   **Ninth overall**
The most obvious example of a first rounder who almost re-entered the draft was Eric Lindros. Lindros never blinked after boycotting the Quebec Nordiques, his 1991 draft team. After

more than a year of frustration with the future star, Quebec prudently dealt Eric to Philadelphia, preventing Lindros from re-entering the draft the next season. The highest position of a player who re-entered the draft belongs to Nick Boynton, Washington's ninth overall choice in 1997. The Capitals' failed to sign Boynton, who returned to the OHL and won MVP status at the Memorial Cup in 1999. He was Boston's first choice, 21st overall at the 1999 Draft.

1.10   D. Swatches of actual equipment fabric
They're similar to most other hockey trading cards, with cool art work, career stats, brief bio and an action shot of an NHL star, except Be A Player cards periodically include a 1½-inch by ¾-inch patch of fabric affixed to the card back. It might be leather bits of Hall of Famer Gerry Cheevers or Bernie Parent's goalie pads or gloves; or, as in the 2000/2001 edition, the 75-year-old pads of hockey's first great netminder Georges Vezina, who played his last game in 1925. Cutting up Vezina's famous pads into swatches of leather and fabric for sale may be sacrilege to many hockey people who would rather see the pads in the Hockey Hall of Fame, but to card companies it's part of the burgeoning trend in memorabilia collecting that gives everyone a chance to own a bit of hockey antiquity. The idea of including sport-used equipment in trading cards began with NASCAR cards, which featured small pieces of drivers' asbestos suits and bits of the cars' hulls. Soon game-worn gear began appearing in a variety of sports cards, hockey being a prime target to attract a larger collector-base. Only 320 "Vezina pad cards" were issued, giving buyers about a 1:2,400 chance of finding an authentic swatch of the great netminder's famous pads. Some cards contain the actual leather exterior, others have the fabric from inside the pad.

1.11   A. Vancouver won 4–3
In the first meeting since Mark Messier departed Vancouver for New York in 2000, the Canucks defeated the Rangers 4–3.

Vancouver fans at the November 17, 2000, game booed the former captain every time he touched the puck. Were the Canucks intimidated by Messier's presence? "They played with him for three years," said Vancouver coach Marc Crawford before the big showdown. "They are going to want to have bragging rights over Mark. That's probably the biggest compliment we can give to Mark, is playing a very strong game . . . ." Messier was held to one assist in the Rangers' loss, as the Canucks began to establish their own identity in the AM (After Mark) era. "We kind of got caught sitting and waiting for him to do everything and expecting him to do it all," said Vancouver forward Trent Klatt. "With him not here, we can't do that."

1.12 D. The Minnesota Wild

In a strange twist, no one player on the Wild was named team captain for their inaugural season, 2001. In fact, several players were honoured with the captaincy during the course of the year, one captain each month from October and April. First there was Sean O'Donnell, the Wild's most consistent blueliner. Then came Scott Pellerin, the club's leading scorer. Next was Wes Walz, who led Minnesota to a winning record in December. After that defenseman Brad Bombardir wore the "C" in January, and because his play picked up so dramatically, he was assigned the captaincy again in February. Captain of the month was head coach Jacques Lemaire's idea. "We will try to give every player a chance to show their leadership to this hockey club," said Lemaire. "It's working great. I like the impact it has had on the team and especially on the guy who has been named captain."

1.13 C. At Notre Dame Basilica in Old Montreal

French Canada's most beautiful and important church, Notre Dame Basilica, has witnessed many historic events, including the funeral of former Prime Minister Pierre Trudeau and the wedding of pop diva Celine Dion. But few other occasions compare to the funeral mass for Maurice Richard where a who's who of Canadian society and hockey attended the 90-minute service celebrating the Rocket's life and death on May 31, 2000. The funeral, organized by the Montreal Canadiens, was attended by 800 invited guests and 2,200 fans, who filled the second and third floor balconies, some wearing Montreal Canadiens sweaters. Thousands more watched outside and hundreds of thousands on national television. At such an extravaganza, with politicians, hockey legends and family in attendance, what was the seating arrangement? Richard's casket was placed in an aisle between two sections of pews, with immediate family in front of hockey friends on one side and dignitaries on the other. Louis Dussault, counsel to the Canadiens for the Richard funeral, explained to the *National Post* the plan: "...we kept in mind that this was a funeral for a hero, not a politician. So the prime minister, the premier and the mayor were seated in the front row. The second row was reserved for the hockey dignitaries, including NHL Commissioner Gary Bettman. Mr. Mulroney (former prime minister) sat in the third row. Federal cabinet ministers were seated in front of provincial cabinet ministers, but behind provincial party leaders. Trust me—it was all very carefully arranged." Invited journalists such as Don Cherry were placed in the remaining rows behind city councillors.

1.14 A. Ryan Smyth

The odds of repeating such a feat are astronomical, as the NHL record book bears out, but when Ryan Smyth scored all three goals in the Oilers 3–0 win over St. Louis on November 14, 2000, he became the first player in league annals to notch hat tricks in 3–0 games twice. Smyth scored two times in the first period and added an empty-netter in the third to duplicate his previous hat trick performance in a 3–0 victory over Atlanta on March 13, 2000. Smyth's hat trick on November 14 was only the 11th time in the NHL's 83-year history that a player scored all three goals in a 3–0 game.

1.15 D. Five players
With few exceptions, such as the Coloured Hockey League in Atlantic Canada during the early 1900s, hockey has been an almost exclusively white-man's sport. The game's history is peppered with stories of quality black players such as Herb Carnegie and Willie O'Ree and their struggle against the NHL's so-called colour barrier. Then came Tony McKegney and Grant Fuhr, hockey's first legitimate black stars. They opened the door for more young black hockey players and in 2000–01 a record 14 black players were on NHL rosters. After the Anson Carter trade with Boston in 2000, the Edmonton Oilers boosted five blacks, including Carter, Mike Grier, Georges Laraque, Sean Brown and Joaquin Gage. "Every city we go to, black kids are going to look to the five of us," said Laraque. "We are role models for them, and that's a great thing for us." Grier, who is the nephew of NFL great Roosevelt Grier and played in the Ice Hockey In Harlem program, said, "All of us are in a situation where we feel fortunate to have made it."

1.16 B. Doug Jarvis
Wayne Gretzky may be Brantford, Ontario's most famous son, but 30 other players from Gretzky's hometown have made it to the NHL, including Doug Jarvis, the all-time NHL ironman at 964 games. Jarvis, chosen 24th overall in 1975, never missed a single game in 12 seasons and won four Stanley Cups on Montreal's dynasty team in the late 1970s. Yes, Jarvis was once coached by Wayne's dad, Walter Gretzky, in Brantford peewee hockey.

1.17 A. Never
During his 19-year career Scott Stevens has never been a minus—not once. The New Jersey defenseman had a flat zero in 1985–86 and a few plus-1's (1988–89 and 1989–90) during his years in Washington, but with the Devils he's fared better, including a career high and league-leading +53 in 1993–94.

1.18 B. Between 60 and 70 per cent
When the NHL started publishing faceoff stats in the late 1990s, it became clear that the highest winning percentage among the best in the circle is in the mid-60 per cent range. In 1999–2000, Yanic Perreault led the NHL by winning more than 62 per cent of his faceoffs. "To be over 60 per cent is pretty hard," said Perreault in a *Hockey News* story on faceoff battles. "You have to be strong on your stick and you have to be strong on your skates. And you have to try to remember how you've had success against the guys you come up against." Perreault places his bottom hand down low almost to the blade and his top hand slides halfway down the shaft so he positions himself squarely over the blade of the stick. Does he cheat? "Every centre cheats," said Perreault. "You watch the lineman's hand and you try to get the jump. If you see the other centre cheating, you try to cheat first."

1.19 D. Terry Murray
No NHL player has gone longer without scoring a goal in league action than one-time defenseman-turned NHL coach Terry Murray, who played 218 goalless games between 1972–73 (as a member of the California Golden Seals) and 1980–81, when he scored his first (of only four career goals) as a Philadelphia Flyer. It's an accomplishment few remember or will attribute to Murray. Likewise for others in this category, such as tough guy Tony Twist (181 games) or Carolina's Steve Halko, who led all active scoreless players in 2000–01 Halko, in his fourth year with the Hurricanes as a full and part-time NHLer, went 135 NHL games without scoring a single goal. "A couple of times," Halko claimed, "I fired shots that were going into empty nets, but guys tipped them." As of this writing, Halko's last pro goal happened in the AHL in 1998–99.

1.20 A. Harry Mummery
In old-time hockey when a goalie was too badly injured to continue, another player from the team donned his equipment and

replaced him in the net. The first skater to stand in for an injured netminder during an NHL game was Quebec Bulldog defenseman Harry Mummery, who subbed for goalie Frank Brophy three times—February 4, March 8 and March 10, 1920—during the 1919–20 season. But Mummery played a better defensive game manning the blue line than between the pipes. In his three "goalie" games he won one but allowed 18 goals for an awful 7.61 goals-against average. High numbers in any era but not as bad as some nights when number one goalie Frank Brophy backstopped the Bulldogs. On March 3, 1920, a healthy Brophy allowed a record 16 goals in a 16–3 shellacking against the Montreal Canadiens. It is still the NHL record for most goals scored by one team in one game. Mummery subbed one more game on January 21, 1922 when he replaced Hamilton Tiger goalie Howie Lockhart in a 7–6 win against Ottawa. All four games Mummery worked as a substitute goalkeeper were against the old Ottawa Senators.

1.21 D. 2000–01
After Sprague and Odie Cleghorn blasted Hamilton goalie Howie Lockhart for four goals apiece in Montreal's 10–6 whipping over the Tigers in 1922, another 78 years passed before two other teammates duplicated the eight-goal performance in a single game. New Jersey's Randy McKay and John Madden repeated the scoring oddity on October 28, 2000, scoring four goals each against Pittsburgh's Garth Snow and Jean-Sebastien Aubin in the Devils' 9–0 lashing. After learning that McKay and Madden had become the league's first four-goals-apiece teammates since 1922, New Jersey coach Larry Robinson said: "Holy mackerel."

1.22 B. 115 of 261 OT periods
Statistics tell the real success story of the NHL's first season of four-on-four hockey during overtime periods in 1999–2000. Of the 261 extra periods, 115 recorded game-winners, a 44.1 per cent decision rate. In 1998–99, playing five skaters aside in over-

time, only 27 per cent of games did not end tied, with 60 OT goals scored in 222 games. Tied games decreased by 15 per cent, from 166 to 146.

1.23   D. Minnesota
Of the 773 American-born NHLers, 24.2 per cent or 187 players have come from Minnesota, followed by Massachusetts (176 players) 22.8 per cent, Michigan (92 players) 11.9 per cent and New York (80 players) 10.3 per cent.

1.24   B. Toronto
Canada's largest city, Toronto, has sent 373 players to the NHL, followed by Montreal (250), Winnipeg (175) and Edmonton (162). Further demographic analysis (from a 1996 Canadian census) of more than 6,000 NHLers indicate that smaller cities and towns such as Kirkland Lake, Ontario, or Medicine Hat, Alberta, have contributed as much to the development of world class hockey players as the large urban centres. In fact, Canada's three western provinces of Manitoba, Saskatchewan and Alberta have sent 30 per cent of the total of Canadian-born players to the NHL despite accounting for just 16.6 per cent of the country's entire population. Ontario, with 1,999 players, accounts for almost 45 per cent of the league's Canadian population; Quebec (740 players) 16.7 per cent; Alberta (462 players) 10.4 per cent; and Saskatchewan (451 players) 10.2 per cent.

Game 1

"STITCH ME UP, BOYS"

After being horribly slashed in the face by Brad May in November 2000, Columbus' Steve Heinze tersely instructed the Blue Jackets' trainers: "Stitch me up, boys, we're on a power play." Heinze was back out on the ensuing man-advantage and scored the power play goal. May received a 20-game suspension. In this game match the hockey men and their cutting comments.

(Solutions are on page 120)

Jaromir Jagr	Maurice Richard	Patrick Roy
Theoren Fleury	Don Cherry	Claude Lemieux
Steve Ludzik	Mike Milbury	

1. _____ "I've got so much to say, I can't wait to hear myself say it."

2. _____ "What's the "C" stand for—selfish?"

3. _____ "I'll take my (three) rings over his (five) Vezinas."

4. _____ "They should mind their own (bleeping) business and figure out their own problems."

5. _____ "I was awful. Just plain awful"

6. _____ "I'm just a hockey player"

7. _____ "I don't know where my hands are. Maybe I left them in Japan."

8. _____ "He'll chew a goal post apart to put a puck in the net."

2
THE MASKED ART

In the last 30 years, only two NHL goalies have posted all of their teams wins during a season. Kirk McLean was in net for all 18 of the Vancouver Canucks' wins during the lockout-shortened 1994–95 season. Who was the other netminder? In this chapter we strap on the pads for a few high-speed brain busters.

(*Answers are on page 23*)

2.1 Who was the first goalie to score a goal and record a shutout in the same game?
A. Chris Osgood
B. Ron Hextall
C. Jose Theodore
D. Martin Brodeur

2.2 Former NHL goalie Eddie Johnston was the last goalie to play every minute of an NHL season. How many broken noses did he suffer in that perfect season, 1963–64?
A. None
B. One broken nose
C. Two broken noses
D. Four broken noses

2.3 In October 2000 Patrick Roy recorded his 447th win, to tie the great Terry Sawchuk for most career victories in NHL history. Against which team did Patrick Roy collect his most wins?
A. The Montreal Canadiens
B. The Boston Bruins
C. The Carolina Hurricanes/Hartford Whalers
D. The Toronto Maple Leafs

2.4 Who is considered the best goalie (most career wins) to never win the Stanley Cup?

A. Tony Esposito
B. John Vanbiesbrouck
C. Ron Hextall
D. Ed Giacomin

2.5 Which small Canadian town has been the birthplace of no less than 26 NHL goaltenders, including such well-known names as Turk Broda, Ron Hextall, Bill Ranford, Ken Wregget and Glen Hanlon?

A. Weyburn, Saskatchewan
B. Brandon, Manitoba
C. Red Deer, Alberta
D. Kirkland Lake, Ontario

2.6 Among active goalies in 2000–01 who has averaged the best shutout record to games played?

A. Dominik Hasek
B. Martin Brodeur
C. Chris Osgood
D. Patrick Roy

2.7 Who was the first goalie to record a shutout in NHL history?

A. Georges Vezina
B. Chuck Gardiner
C. Lorne Chabot
D. George Hainsworth

2.8 Which NHL goalie collected the most shutouts in his rookie season?

A. Terry Sawchuk
B. Glenn Hall
C. Tony Esposito
D. Ken Dryden

2.9 Most future NHL greats are spotted early in their careers by scouts. But that's not always the case. Which star netminder was not drafted as a junior?

A. Patrick Roy
B. Ed Belfour
C. Olaf Kolzig
D. Martin Brodeur

2.10 Kirk McLean of Vancouver was the most recent goalie to collect all of his team's wins (18) in 1994–95. Prior to McLean, who was the last NHL goalie to do it in a full season?

A. Ron Low of the 1974–75 Washington Capitals
B. Gary Smith of the 1973–74 Vancouver Canucks
C. Ed Giacomin of the 1966–67 New York Rangers
D. Roger Crozier of the 1964–65 Detroit Red Wings

2.11 Which goalie at the start of 2000–01 was promoted by his team as a potential U.S. presidential candidate during the 2000 American election?

A. Columbus' Ron Tugnutt
B. New York's Mike Richter
C. Florida's Trevor Kidd
D. Atlanta's Damian Rhodes

2.12 How many career shutouts did Dominik Hasek record before he netted his first against the lowly New York Islanders?

A. Hasek's first NHL shutout was against the Islanders
B. Six shutouts
C. 26 shutouts
D. 46 shutouts

2.13 In 1999–2000, the NHL created a new annual award to honour the goalie with the league's best save percentage. The award was named after which former netminder?
A. Glenn Hall
B. Ed Giacomin
C. Roger Crozier
D. Bernie Parent

2.14 Who holds the NHL mark for most wins by a rookie goaltender?
A. Terry Sawchuk
B. Tony Esposito
C. Ed Belfour
D. Martin Brodeur

2.15 Among active goalies in 2000–01, who has the most career losses?
A. Patrick Roy
B. Tom Barrasso
C. Kirk McLean
D. John Vanbiesbrouck

2.16 Which goalie allowed Bobby Orr's classic Stanley Cup-winning goal of 1970? (In the well-known photo of the goal Orr is caught airborne celebrating the Cup-winner.)
A. Jacques Plante
B. Glenn Hall
C. Tony Esposito
D. Ed Giacomin

2.17 How many protective cups does Detroit goalie Manny Legace wear in NHL games?
A. None, Legace goes al fresco
B. Legace wears a player's cup
C. Legace wears a goalie's cup
D. Legace wears two cups

2.18 The 2000 Stanley Cup finals pitted goalie Martin Brodeur of the New Jersey Devils against Ed Belfour of the Dallas Stars. Both were former rookies of the year. When was the last time prior to 2000 the Cup finals featured two netminders who had won Calder Trophies?

A. 1950
B. 1973
C. 1992
D. It had not happened before

2.19 Patrick Roy passed Terry Sawchuk as the NHL's winningest goalie during the 2000–01 season. But if minor-league wins are included in the total, which goalie posted the most victories in pro hockey history?

A. Terry Sawchuk
B. Jacques Plante
C. Johnny Bower
D. Gerry Cheevers

THE MASKED ART
Answers

2.1 **C. Jose Theodore**

As of 2000–01, six netminders have scored goals in the NHL, but Jose Theodore is the only backstopper to score while picking up a shutout. "I couldn't believe it," Theodore said. "Guys like Hextall and Brodeur can think about scoring but I can only dream about it. I don't really have a good shot." Theodore insists he wasn't trying to score when he flipped the puck at the empty net late in the game against the New York Islanders on January 2, 2001. But it kept rolling towards the Islanders' net and sealed Montreal's 3–0 victory. "I just wanted to clear the puck down the middle. If you aim for the boards, there's always the chance of a penalty.... When I saw the puck sliding towards the goal—and I did have time to watch it—it was an extraordinary feeling," Theodore said.

2.2   D. Four broken noses
Eddie Johnston played all 70 games in 1963–64, the last goalie with a perfect attendance record of every minute of every game in a season. But his pain threshold was tested time and again. Johnston suffered four broken noses, maybe an NHL record. Further, his eyes were so swollen from shots, on two occasions doctors applied leeches to suck the blood so he could see well enough to play.

2.3   C. The Carolina Hurricanes/Hartford Whalers
After tying Terry Sawchuk's 30-year league record for career wins on October 14, 2000, hockey historians and statisticians couldn't wait to analyze Roy's path to glory. Of his 447 victories, almost half (44 per cent) or 194 occurred at the Montreal Forum/ Molson Centre; 141 happened on a Saturday; 35 came against Carolina/Hartford; 43 were shutouts; and another five from scoreless ties. Roy beat 90 head coaches, 122 opposing goalies and won games in 40 NHL arenas to reach Sawchuk's milestone 447th. He won nine NHL player-of-the-week awards, his ninth honour coming the week he notched No. 447.

2.4   B. John Vanbiesbrouck
Because long-time Chicago netminder Tony Esposito is fourth on the NHL's all-time wins list with 423 victories, his name is usually chosen first in this category, even by some hockey experts. In fact, Esposito, whose career spanned 16 seasons and 15 as a Blackhawk, won a championship with his first NHL team, the Stanley Cup-winning Montreal Canadiens of 1968–69. Before being claimed by Chicago in the Intra-League Draft in 1969, Espo played 13 regular-season games with Montreal, enough to qualify for a spot on Stanley's silverware. As of February 2000–01, the most-frustrated active goalie was John Vanbiesbrouck, who is Cup-less after 366 regular-season wins. The closest Beezer came to sniffing a championship was in 1996 when his Florida Panthers were swept by Colorado in the Cup finals.

2.5   B. Brandon, Manitoba

Brandon is known for producing two things: wheat and goalies. Despite a population of less than 40,000, the little prairie town has sent an amazing 26 netminders to the NHL. The five goalies mentioned in our question—Turk Broda, Ron Hextall, Bill Ranford, Ken Wregget and Glen Hanlon—combined for 2,936 NHL games, 1,230 wins, 122 shutouts and eight Stanley Cup rings.

2.6   A. Dominik Hasek

The Dominator scores a perfect 10 when it comes to shutouts, averaging a shutout every 10 games during his career.

THE NHL'S BEST SHUTOUT AVERAGES IN 2000

Goalie	GP	SO	Frequency
Dominik Hasek	450	45	1 every 10 games
Martin Brodeur	448	42	1 every 11 games
Chris Osgood	339	29	1 every 12 games
Ed Belfour	615	49	1 every 13 games
Nikolai Khabibulin	284	21	1 every 14 games
Arturs Irbe	398	24	1 every 17 games

Current to 1999-2000/Courtesy of The Hockey News

2.7   A. Georges Vezina

Georges Vezina became the first netminder to record a shutout on February 18th, 1918 when the Montreal Canadiens defeated the Toronto Arenas in a 9–0 bombing. It was the 29th game of the NHL's first season as a league. Vezina joined the Canadiens of the National Hockey Association in 1910–11 and didn't miss a game for 15 years, playing a remarkable 367 consecutive regular-season and playoffs games. After his death of tuberculosis in 1926 the

Montreal Canadiens donated the Vezina Trophy to honour his memory. Vezina was one of the original 12 men elected to the Hockey Hall of Fame.

2.8 **C. Tony Esposito**
After just 13 games and a Stanley Cup with Montreal in 1968–69, Tony Esposito moved to Chicago the following season and proved his No. 1 status by establishing the NHL benchmark for shutouts. Esposito bagged a modern-day record 15 zeroes in 1969–70, his rookie NHL season. He was named to the First All-Star Team, won the Calder Trophy as top rookie and the Vezina Trophy as best goalie.

ROOKIE SHUTOUT KINGS

Player	Team	Year	GP	SO
Tony Esposito	Chicago	1969–70	63	15
George Hainsworth	Montreal	1926–27	44	14
Tiny Thompson	Boston	1928–29	44	12
Glenn Hall	Detroit	1955–56	70	12
Terry Sawchuk	Detroit	1950–51	70	11
Lorne Chabot	NYR	1926–27	36	10
Dolly Dolson	Detroit	1928–29	44	10
Frank Brimsek	Boston	1938–39	43	10

Current to 2000-01

2.9 **B. Ed Belfour**
A Stanley Cup winner with the Dallas Stars in 1999, Ed Belfour is one of the best goalies to appear from nowhere. A native of Carman, Manitoba, Belfour played his junior hockey for the Winkler Flyers in the low-profile Manitoba Junior Hockey League. Ignored by NHL scouts, Belfour was never drafted as a junior. He later signed as a free agent by the Chicago Blackhawks,

whose scouts obviously caught the Eagle's standout season with the NCAA's University of North Dakota Fighting Sioux in 1986–87.

2.10   A.   Ron Low of the 1974–75 Washington Capitals

Teams no longer rely on one goalie as they did back in the 1950s and 1960s, making it difficult for a netminder to get credit for all his club's wins in a season. Still, since the 1960s several goalies have come close: Tony Esposito recorded 25 of the Chicago Blackhawks' 26 wins in 1976–77; Rogie Vachon posted 32 of the Los Angeles Kings' 33 victories that same year; Denis Herron got 11 of the Kansas City Scouts' 12 wins in 1975–76; and Gary Smith backstopped the California Golden Seals to 19 of their 20 wins in 1970–71. But only one netminder since the 1960s has accounted for all his team's wins over a full season. The honour belongs to Ron Low, who notched all eight victories posted by the woeful Washington Capitals in 1974–75. Low's record was 8–36–2. The other Caps' netminders that year—Michel Belhumeur and John Adams—combined for 0-31-3.

MODERN-DAY GOALIES WITH ALL TEAM WINS

Goalie	Year	Team	Wins
Kirk McLean	1994–95[*]	Vancouver	18
Ron Low	1974–75	Washington	8
Cesare Maniago	1968–69	North Stars	18
Ed Giacomin	1966–67	NYR	30
Roger Crozier	1964–65	Detroit	40
Ed Johnston	1963–64	Boston	18

* 48-game schedule / Current to 2000-01

2.11   A.   Columbus' Ron Tugnutt

The Blue Jackets launched their inaugural season, 2000–01, with a great start and Tugnutt played a bigger role than anybody else on the expansion team. In one seven-game stretch during the American presidential race, Tugnutt went 5–1–1 with a hot 1.71 goals-against average and a .945 save percentage. The streak prompted Columbus' marketing department to sell Tugnutt as a presidential candidate in Ohio. Canadian-born Tugnutt is from Scarborough, Ontario.

2.12 D. 46 shutouts
Dominik Hasek shut out at least 20 teams including power-houses such as Colorado, Dallas and St. Louis before he was able to get a zero against the long-struggling Islanders on November 9, 2000. The 3–0 Buffalo win on November 9, 2000, was Hasek's 46th career shutout. He faced just 22 shots. The victory helped him improve his feeble 5–11–5 record against New York.

2.13 C. Roger Crozier
The newly-created MBNA Roger Crozier Saving Grace Award includes a trophy and a $25,000 cash award to be donated to a youth hockey or educational program of the winner's choice. Ed Belfour won the inaugural award with a .919 save percentage in 1999–2000. Roger Crozier, the goalie whose name dignifies the award, was one of the NHL's top goaltenders during a 14-year career (1963 to 1977) spent with Detroit, Buffalo and Washington. He won the Calder Trophy as the league's top rookie in 1965, and in 1966 he became the first goalie to capture the Conn Smythe Trophy as MVP of the playoffs. After his retirement Crozier worked with the company that sponsors the award, the MBNA American Bank. He died of cancer in 1996.

2.14 A. Terry Sawchuk
Terry Sawchuk wasted no time establishing himself as an NHL star. The freshman goalie took the league by storm, recording 44 wins, 11 shutouts and a 1.99 goals-against average, as he led the Detroit Red Wings to a first-place finish in 1950-51. Sawchuk's 44 victories set an NHL record for wins by a goalie that has since

been surpassed by only one other netminder: Bernie Parent, who posted 47 for the Philadelphia Flyers in 1973–74. Ed Belfour narrowly missed equalling Sawchuk's rookie standard when he notched 43 wins for Chicago in 1990–91.

2.15   D. John Vanbiesbrouck

John Vanbiesbrouck owns the title no goalie is after: most losses by an active goalie in 2000–01. To date Vanbiesbrouck has amassed a record 341 losses in 867 games since 1983-84. Among all goalies in NHL history, Beezer is creeping up on the all-time leader in losses, Gump Worsley, who piled up 352 losses in 861 games between 1952 and 1974.

THE NHL'S TOP FIVE ACTIVE GOALIES WITH MOST LOSSES*

Goalie	First Season	Games	Losses
John Vanbiesbrouck	1983–84	867	341
Patrick Roy	1985–86	886	273
Tom Barrasso	1983–84	733	259
Kirk McLean	1987–88	606	259
Sean Burke	1987–88	620	273

*Active in 2000-01
Current to February 2001/Courtesy of The Hockey News

2.16   B.   Glenn Hall

It may be the most famous photo in the history of the NHL. Bobby Orr, frozen by the camera lens of Ray Lussier, is sailing through mid-air, his hands outstretched in celebration after scoring Boston's Stanley Cup-winner just 40 seconds in overtime against St. Louis's Glenn Hall on May 10, 1970. Orr had just finished off a give-and-go with teammate Derek Sanderson and, as he fired point blank on Hall, Orr had his skates taken out from beneath him by Blues defenseman Noel Picard. "I told Bobby a couple of times that I had already showered before he landed. I also asked him if that was the only goal he ever scored. I mean, he and I must have autographed a zillion of those pictures people brought to him," said Hall on the 30th anniversary of Orr's goal in May 2000.

2.17 D. Two cups
Prior to the 1994 Olympics in Lillehammer, Canadian goalie Manny Legace took a shot in a sensitive area at practice. "Oh yeah, I took a slapshot right in the balls," Lagace told the *National Post*. "Oh yeah. Kept me out for a week and a half. That's when I went to two cups. Oh yeah. Slapshot from like four or five feet away, I just went down...I wear two. A player's cup and a regular goalie cup." Legace recovered in time for the Olympics and still sports two cups in his NHL career.

2.18 C. 1992
The appearance of two goalies with Calder Trophy credentials in the Stanley Cup finals is surprisingly rare today but was a frequent occurrence during the 1960s when a handful of net-minders dominated the NHL. In that era Calder winners Terry Sawchuk (1951), Gump Worsley (1953), Glenn Hall (1956) and Roger Crozier (1965) faced off against one another in various combinations during five Cup finals, 1961, 1966, 1967, 1968 and 1969. In the 1973 finals former Calder recipients Ken Dryden (1972) of Montreal and Chicago's Tony Esposito (1970) squared off for the championship. It was the second time the pair had met in the Cup finals. They also met in 1971, but at that point Dryden had not yet won his Calder. The seventh time rookies of the year challenged for the Cup was in 1992 when Ed Belfour (1991) met Tom Barrasso (1984) in finals action, the last time prior to the Martin Brodeur–Ed Belfour matchup of 2000.

2.19 C. Johnny Bower

Johnny Bower won 250 NHL games, which ranks far behind Patrick Roy's total of 473 atop the all-time list. However, Bower did not play his first NHL game until the age of 29, after toiling eight years in the minors. By the time he gained steady employment in the NHL, Bower had 359 wins in the American Hockey League and 30 more in the Western Hockey League. If you add those pro victories to his NHL total (and include playoffs), Bower can claim 706 wins, about 100 more than Roy and 17 more than Jacques Plante, who ranks second on the all-time list.

GOALTENDERS' ALL-TIME PRO WINS

Goalie	League and Wins						
	NHL	AHL	WHL	WHA	Others	Playoffs	Total
Johnny Bower	250	359	30	0	0	67	706
Jacques Plante	435	51	0	15	108	80	689
Gump Worsley	335	79	78	0	58	70	620
Terry Sawchuk	446	69	0	0	30	63	608
Patrick Roy	473	1	0	0	0	131	605
Glenn Hall	407	22	94	0	0	77	600

Current to February 2001

Game 2

THE SHOOTING GALLERY

In this game the names of 39 NHL goaltenders listed below appear in the puzzle, horizontally, vertically, diagonally and even backwards. Some are quickly found, like Curtis JOSEPH; others require a more careful search. After you've circled all 39 names, read the remaining letters in descending order to spell the South Africa-born netminder who won the Vezina Trophy as top goalie in 1999–2000.

(Solutions are on page 120)

AUBIN	BELFOUR	BIRON
BOUCHER	BRATHWAITE	BURKE
BRODEUR	CLOUTIER	DAFOE
DUNHAM	ESSENSA	FISET
HACKETT	HASEK	HEBERT
IRBE	JOSEPH	KIDD
LALIME	MARACLE	OSGOOD
POTVIN	RHODES	RICHTER
ROY SALO	SHIELDS	SNOW
STORR	TALLAS	THEODORE
THIBAULT	TUGNUTT	TUREK
VERNON	VOKOUN	WEEKES
WREGGET	VANBIESBROUCK	

```
B V E J M A H N U D O O G S O
N O A R O P E Y O R H O D E S
I K U N O S O B E M I L A L E
B O I C B D E T R K E R U T O
U U O D H I O P V I W L R T F
A N A F D E E E H I O T E L A
B E L F O U R S H K N T I U D
T R U E D O R B B B T S U T A E
E H E B E R T B I R O N U B L
G O L N O N R E V Z O G O I C
G E I T R I C H T E R U L H A
E K S E T T E K C A H T C T R
R R A S A L L A T H A S E K A
W U L I B R A T H W A I T E M
G B O F A S N E S S E K E E W
```

3
TIES THAT BIND

What is the highest number of 100-point teams in one regular season in NHL history? Typically, NHL regular seasons produce three or four 100-point teams, or, on occasion, five century-point clubs in one year. But twice in league annals, seven teams have amassed 100 points or more during the regular season: first, in 1992–93, when the NHL played its first ever 84-game schedule; and, then, in 1999–2000's 82-game season. In this chapter, its team chemistry, on and off the ice.

(Answers are on page 38)

3.1 As of 2000–01, which NHL team is considered to be the best at drafting European talent?
A. The Pittsburgh Penguins
B. The Montreal Canadiens
C. The Ottawa Senators
D. The Detroit Red Wings

3.2 Who is the only Bruin in modern-day hockey to lead Boston in goals, assists, points and penalty minutes in one season?
A. Bobby Orr
B. Terry O'Reilly
C. Cam Neely
D. Joe Thornton

3.3 What is the most number of shorthanded goals scored by one team in a season?
A. 16 shorthanded goals
B. 26 shorthanded goals
C. 36 shorthanded goals
D. 46 shorthanded goals

3.4 Which team has the worst record in season openers?
A. The New York Islanders
B. The Mighty Ducks of Anaheim
C. The Toronto Maple Leafs
D. The Dallas Stars

3.5 What is the least number of shorthanded goals scored by an entire team in a season?
A. Zero shorthanded goals
B. Five shorthanded goals
C. 10 shorthanded goals
D. 15 shorthanded goals

3.6 What is the most number of teams a NHL rookie of the year played on before capturing the Calder Trophy as top rookie?
A. Two teams
B. Three teams
C. Four teams
D. Five teams

3.7 In a five-year span between 1996 and 2000, how many players drafted by Montreal have found steady employment (minimum 150 games in five seasons) in the NHL?
A. None
B. Five players
C. 10 players
D. 15 players

3.8 The New York-Brooklyn Americans folded in 1942, beginning the NHL's legendary six-team era. In what year did the last American player play in the NHL?
A. 1942
B. 1949
C. 1952
D. 1959

3.9 How many years elapsed between the old North Stars franchise and the new Wild in Minnesota?
A. Three years
B. Five years
C. Seven years
D. Nine years

3.10 What is the most number of consecutive wins posted by an expansion team in its first year?
A. Two straight wins
B. Three straight wins
C. Four straight wins
D. Five straight wins

3.11 What is the most number of regular-season games one NHL team played before registering its first penalty shot in franchise history? (Name the team.)
A. Fewer than 400 games
B. Between 400 and 600 games
C. Between 600 and 800 games
D. More than 800 games

3.12 Which team recorded the best penalty-killing average in NHL history?
A. The New Jersey Devils in 1994–95
B. The Washington Capitals in 1997–98
C. The Boston Bruins in 1998–99
D. The Dallas Stars in 1999–2000

3.13 Which NHL team started a season with two black goalies as their No. 1 and No. 2 netminders?
A. The Edmonton Oilers
B. The Calgary Flames
C. The St. Louis Blues
D. The Boston Bruins

3.14 What is the lowest number of shots recorded by one NHL team in one period?

A. Zero shots

B. One shot

C. Two shots

D. Three shots

3.15 What is the fewest number of games needed by a team to reach 40 points from the start of a season?

A. 21 games

B. 23 games

C. 25 games

D. 27 games

3.16 How many former Minnesota North Stars were still playing for the Dallas Stars when the Stars returned for the first time to play the Wild in Minnesota in 2000–01?

A. Only one, Mike Modano

B. Three players

C. Five players

D. Seven players

3.17 Two Toronto Maple Leaf players with the same sweater number recorded the club's best finishes in individual scoring since 1960. What is that jersey number?

A. No. 10

B. No. 14

C. No. 22

D. No. 27

3.18 If you were reading the sports pages in 1917, the year
the NHL first formed, you would find the names of
only two current NHL teams listed in the standings.
Which two?
A. The Montreal Canadiens and the Ottawa Senators
B. The Montreal Canadiens and the Toronto Maple Leafs
C. The Montreal Canadiens and the Boston Bruins
D. The Montreal Canadiens and the New York Rangers

3.19 How much time passed between Dallas's controversial
1999 Stanley Cup win in Buffalo and the next Stars-Sabres
game at the HSBC Arena in Buffalo?
A. 200 to 300 days
B. 300 to 400 days
C. 400 to 500 days
D. More than 500 days

3.20 Which expansion team set an NHL attendance record for most
fans in its first season?
A. The San Jose Sharks in 1991–92
B. The Tampa Bay Lightning in 1992–93
C. The Mighty Ducks of Anaheim of 1993–94
D. The Atlanta Thrashers of 1999–2000

TIES THAT BIND
Answers

3.1 C. **The Ottawa Senators**
Nobody drafts better in Europe than the Ottawa Senators. Their
long-term commitment to building through the draft turned a
weak expansion franchise into a club stockpiled with quality
talent, much of it due to their scouting operations in Europe.
Ottawa hit pay dirt with premium draft picks such as Alexei
Yashin (second overall–1992), Radek Bonk (third overall–1994)
and Marian Hossa (12th overall–1997), but they have consis-

tently unearthed mid-round European finds in the likes of Daniel Alfredsson (133rd–1994), Pavol Demitra (227th–1993), Andreas Dackell (136th–1996), Magnus Arvedson (119th–1997) and Sami Salo (239th–1996). A lot of the credit belongs to Senators general manager Marshall Johnson, who was once director of player personnel in charge of the draft.

3.2   D. Joe Thornton

Joe Thornton created little noise in his first two seasons after being selected first overall by Boston in 1997. But in his third year, he began proving what the scouts had predicted all along for the 6-foot-four, 220-pound centre. In 1999–2000 he led Boston in goals, assists, points and penalty minutes with a 23–37–60 record and 82 minutes in box time. His feat may have as much to do with Thornton the player as with the Bruins, a team scarce on talent. Nonetheless, considering the situation in Boston, his 60 points is an achievement; and something no other Bruin—not Orr, Esposito or Neely—has done, dating back 76 years to Boston's first season, 1924–25, when centre Jimmy Herbert recorded team-leading goals, assists, points and penalty minutes for the "B's." Thornton was the only NHLer in 1999–2000 to lead his club in both scoring and penalty minutes.

3.3   C. 36 shorthanded goals

No team in NHL history has matched the offensive numbers of the Edmonton Oilers during the 1980s. In fact, during Edmonton's most productive season, 1983–84, losing a man to the penalty box actually helped on occasion. Of the record 446 Oiler goals that season, 36 were scored while Edmonton was a man short. Wayne Gretzky was the biggest benefactor of more ice space (even if it was at the expense of a fellow Oiler), notching 12 shorthanders or 33 per cent of Edmonton's record man-disadvantage output. The Oilers also hold down the next three best league marks in this category with 28 shorthanded goals in 1986–87 and 27 goals in 1985–86 and 1988–89. Surprisingly, when it comes to the man advantage goals on the power-play, Edmonton doesn't even rank among the top four goal-scoring teams in NHL history.

3.4   B.   The Mighty Ducks of Anaheim

The worst record for season-openers belongs to Anaheim, a team of Mighty Ducks with the league's nastiest case of stage fright. Their first opening night victory in franchise history—a 3–1 win over the Minnesota Wild—came on October 6, 2000, the start of their eighth season since joining the NHL in 1993. Duck fans provided another first as only 16,520 attended the game, some 640 short of capacity. It marked the club's first non-sell-out on opening night. In debut wins-losses Anaheim has an abysmal .125 winning percentage in eight attempts.

WORST RECORDS IN SEASON OPENERS

Team	GP	W	L	T	Pct.
Anaheim	8	1	7	0	.125
San Jose	10	2	6	2	.300
Carolina	22	5	12	5	.341
Islanders	29	7	14	8	.379
Toronto	84	32	38	14	.464

Current to 2000–01

3.5   A.   Zero shorthanded goals

How bad a year did Boston have in 1999–2000, a season in which they distinguished themselves with almost no offense on their way to a miserable 24–39–19 record? Things were so difficult in Beantown that the best (or worst) bit of trivia we could gleam from their team stats pertained to shorthanded goals: zero. The Bruins were the only NHL team to go zip in this category in 1999–2000.

3.6 **B. Three teams**
The NHL's first Calder Trophy winner, Carl Voss, was on his third
NHL team by the time he won the top rookie award in 1933. Voss
played just 14 games with Toronto over two seasons (1926–27
and 1928–29) before he returned to the NHL in 1932–33 to play
a full 48-game schedule, split between the New York Rangers
(10 games) and the Detroit Red Wings (38 games). Voss scored
23 points as rookie of the year. Other players such as Pentti Lund
(Boston and New York), Tony Esposito (Montreal and Chicago),
Danny Grant (Montreal and Minnesota) each played on two
teams before their Calder win.

3.7 **A. None**
The Montreal Canadiens, long known for their astute appraisal of
talent and team building through draft picks, were run into the
ground during the 1990s after several years of backward thinking
in their scouting operations. Montreal ignored the European
potential, favouring tough guys who couldn't skate and Quebec-
born players to please the fans. Unfortunately, not one player
selected between 1996 and 2000 had found steady work (minimum 150 games) in the NHL before the start of 2000–01. (Brett
Clark, Montreal's 7th choice in 1996, had 116 games; and
Russian-born Andrei Markov, Montreal's sixth pick in 1998, began
play with the Canadiens in 2000–01.) Worse, the only player of
premium consequence selected by the Canadiens in a 12-year span
was injury-prone Saku Koivu. The Habs aren't alone when it comes
to scouting problems. Only a few players—such as Steve McCarty
(five games) and Daniel Cleary (58 games)—drafted by Chicago
between 1996 and 2000 had cracked an NHL roster as of 2000–01.

3.8 **D. 1959**
Even though the New York Americans preceded the Rangers in
the NHL, it was the Rangers who became Broadway's most popular hockey team. The Americans never attained the lustre
accorded their cross-town rivals, functioning as the league's retire-

ment home for many past-their-prime NHL veterans. A few stars did emerge however, including Kenny Mosdell and Harry Watson, both of whom began their NHL careers in the Americans' last season, 1941–42. Mosdell and Watson were regulars until 1957, but Kenny played three playoff games in 1959 for Montreal, replacing the injured Jean Beliveau and earning the distinction of being the last New York American in NHL play.

3.9 C. Seven years
Minnesota hockey fans waited seven long years for a new club after owner Norm Green moved their beloved North Stars to Dallas in 1993. The wait ended on October 11, 2000 when the Wild played their first home game before a full house of 18,827 at Xcel Energy Center in St. Paul. Fittingly, the first home-game goal was scored by winger Darby Hendrickson, who grew up in suburban Richfield and played at the University of Minnesota. "It was unbelievable," Hendrickson said in *The Hockey News.* "There was so much history here tonight and I'm just thankful to be part of it." To top the evening, the Wild recorded its first point in club history, playing to a 3–3 tie against the Philadelphia Flyers.

3.10 C. Four straight wins
As of 2000–01, nine expansion teams have tied the NHL record for consecutive wins in their first season. The Columbus Blue Jackets became the ninth first-year club to win four straight after defeating San Jose (5–2) on November 9th, Phoenix (2–1) on November 11th, Dallas (3–2) on November 14th and Nashville (5–1) on November 16th. Columbus' bubble burst in the fifth game after a 3–0 loss against Florida on November 17th. Prior to the Blue Jackets, the last expansion club to win four-in-a-row was the 1993–94 first-year Panthers.

3.11 D. More than 800 games
The New Jersey franchise played in 829 regular-season games (as the Devils, Kansas City Scouts and Colorado Rockies) before

recording its first penalty shot, the longest wait in NHL history. The historic shot came on December 17, 1984, as Rocky Trottier scored one-on-one against Edmonton's Andy Moog at the Meadowlands. The Devils' first penalty shot goal was also the first goal ever allowed in a penalty shot situation in Oilers history. Among expansion teams since 1990, Anaheim waited the longest to record a penalty shot. The Mighty Ducks took 315 games before Joe Sacco's goal on November 12, 1997.

3.12 D. The Dallas Stars in 1999–2000
Dallas posted the best penalty-killing average in NHL history when they allowed just 33 power-play goals in 307 short-handed situations for a 89.3 per cent success rate in 1999–2000. The Stars, boasting some of the league's best shot-blockers and defensive specialists, eclipsed both Boston in 1998–99 and Washington in 1997–98 as each finished with a 89.2 penalty-killing percentage.

3.13 B. The Calgary Flames
In 1999–2000 the Flames made NHL history icing the first black tandem ever to start a season with goalies Grant Fuhr and Fred Brathwaite as the No. 1 and No. 2 netminders. In 1989–90 Edmonton had two black goalies on the roster, Fuhr and Eldon (Pokey) Reddick, but they were No. 2 and No. 3 behind starter Bill Ranford.

3.14 A. Zero shots
NHL teams are seldom held shotless through 20 minutes, but it happens, even to the best clubs. On December 2, 2000, the powerhouse Detroit Red Wings were outshot 20–0 in the first period by the Tampa Bay Lightning. The Lightning scored three times, none of them on any of the five power plays given up by Detroit in the first frame. The Red Wings roared back doubling Tampa Bay's shot output in the second and third periods, but Dan Cloutier stoned Detroit, earning his first career shutout 3–0

before 20,718 fans, the largest crowd for a hockey game in Tampa's Ice Palace. The shotless period was the first one since at least 1960 for the Wings; the Lightning held the New York Islanders without a shot in the third period of their game on February 15, 1994.

3.15 B. 23 games
When the Colorado Avalanche blew out of the starting gate in 2000–01 with an 11-game unbeaten streak and recorded a league-best 19–4–3 mark in 26 games, they were only fast enough for seventh place in league history to reach 40 points. No team has had a better season start than Boston in 1929–30 when the Bruins won 20 of their first 23 games, mostly on the Vezina Trophy-winning performance of goalie Tiny Thompson. Thompson lost only five games all season, leading the NHL with 38 wins in the 44-game schedule.

THE NHL'S QUICKEST 40 POINT EARNERS

Team	Year	Win	Loss	Tie	GP
Boston	1929–30	20	3	0	23
Montreal	1943–44	19	2	3	24
Montreal	1927–28	18	2	4	24
Philadelphia	1979–80	17	1	6	24
Edmonton	1983–84	19	3	2	24
Edmonton	1984–85	19	3	3	25
Colorado	2000–01	19	4	3	26

Current to 2000–01

3.16 B. Three players
When the Stars returned to Minnesota for the first time since their move to Dallas (except for one neutral site game) in 1993, only three players from the original Minnesota team survived: Mike Modano, Derian Hatcher and Richard Matvichuk. In the

December 17, 2000, game the Wild won their most lopsided victory to date waxing the Stars 6–0 before a record crowd of 18,834. Three of the Wild's six goals were scored by Minnosota natives: Jeff Neilsen (1) and Darby Hendrickson (2).

3.17 D. No. 27
As of 2000–01 no Toronto player has won the Art Ross Trophy as regular-season scoring leader since Gord Drillon captured the award in 1938. The best any Leaf has done in scoring in the last half-century (since Max Bentley's third-place in 1950–51) is two third-place finishes, both by No. 27s, Frank Mahovlich with 84 points in 1960–61 and Darryl Sittler with 117 points in 1977–78.

3.18 A. The Montreal Canadiens and the Ottawa Senators
The NHL that began play in 1917 consisted of four Canadian teams: the Canadiens and the Senators, and the Montreal Wanderers and the Toronto Arenas (or Blue Shirts, as they were commonly known). The Arenas, who won the Cup that first season, would later change their name to the St. Patricks, before becoming the Maple Leafs in 1927. After winning four Stanley Cups, the original Senators franchise folded in 1931, only to be reborn as an expansion team in 1992–93.

3.19 D. More than 500 days
After Dallas won the 1999 Stanley Cup on Brett Hull's controversial foot-in-the-crease overtime goal in Buffalo on June 19, 1999, the Stars didn't returned to Buffalo until November 15, 2000; or 514 days after their Cup victory. Buffalo and Dallas met only once in 1999–2000, a 3–1 Sabre victory at the Dr. Pepper StarCenter. Dallas' return to Buffalo ended in a 2–2 tie. Asked if the wounds had healed after so long, Sabres coach Lindy Ruff said: "I don't think so." The Stars' Mike Keane shared no sympathy for Buffalo fans, saying: "Our names are on the Cup, and we don't worry about it."

3.20 D. The Atlanta Thrashers of 1999–2000

Fans were easier to come by than wins for the Thrashers in 1999–2000. Atlanta set an expansion team record by averaging 17,205 fans per game in their first season, including 14 sellouts. But audience loyalty brought few victories as the Thrashers challenged league standards for futility in the win column with a 14–61–7 record. The mark was the fourth-worst record for an expansion club since 1970, the fourth highest loss total ever and second most defeats at home (29). "It's been a hard year," lamented goalie Damian Rhodes.

Game 3

THE EURO DRAFTEE

The first Europeans drafted into North American hockey during the 1970s have gained little prominence over the years compared to their successors, the Swedes, Czechs and Russians in today's game. Yesterday's Euro picks remain virtually nameless in the league record books despite being the first of their nationality to earn a NHL draft position. In this game match the European draftee in the left column and his NHL "first" in the right column.

(Solutions are on page 120)

1. _____ Tommi Salmalainen A. First European chosen in first round, 1976

2. _____ Per Alexandersson B. First Swedish draft pick, 1974

3. _____ Viktor Khatulev C. First European selected first overall, 1989

4. _____ Bjorn Johansson D. First Czechoslovak draft pick, 1978

5. _____ Ladislav Svozil E. First German draft pick, 1978

6. _____ Bernhard Englbrecht F. First Russian draft pick, 1975

7. _____ Mats Sundin G. First European draft pick, 1969

4
PRINCES OF PAIN

After serving his 20-game suspension for slashing Columbus' Steve Heinze in the face, tough guy Brad May roared back on January 4, 2001, and set up the game winner by drawing a Rangers' penalty—a retaliatory move for a punishing hit by May near the New York bench. "Brad's the one who stirs the pot," said coach Bob Francis. "He gets everyone's attention, they forget about paying attention to detail and the puck winds up in the net." In this chapter we draw some attention of our own to the top heavyweights—the NHL's princes of pain.

(Answers are on page 52)

4.1 What is the longest suspension for an on-ice incident in NHL history?
A. 13 games
B. 18 games
C. 23 games
D. 28 games

4.2 Which former NHL tough guy sued Spawn Comics and HBO, originally winning US$24.5 million in a lawsuit for misuse of his name?
A. Dave "Tiger" Williams
B. Tony Twist
C. Dale Hunter
D. Dave "The Hammer" Schultz

4.3 Which NHL scrapper was told by the league to drop his hand-wiping act after winning a fight in 2000–01?
A. Donald Brashear
B. Tie Domi

C. Matthew Barnaby
D. Chris Simon

4.4 Which old-time NHL penalty leader was nicknamed "Box-Car" because he spent so much time in the penalty box?
A. Pat Egan
B. Gus Mortson
C. Lou Fontinato
D. John Ferguson

4.5 What is the most number of stitches required to sew up a player's face after an on-ice injury?
A. Fewer than 100 stitches
B. Between 100 and 150 stitches
C. Between 150 and 200 stitches
D. More than 200 stitches

4.6 Which NHL penalty-minute leader recorded the most goals in the season that he led the league in PIM?
A. Maurice Richard
B. Ted Lindsay
C. Bob Probert
D. Dave Williams

4.7 What was bruiser Chris Simon's goal count over seven NHL seasons before he scored a personal-best 29 goals in 1999–2000?
A. 43 goals
B. 63 goals
C. 83 goals
D. 103 goals

4.8 Which defenseman sidelined Eric Lindros with his sixth concussion during the 2000 playoffs?

A. Chris Pronger
B. Scott Stevens
C. Ken Daneyko
D. Darius Kasparaitus

4.9 How much time spanned the six concussions Eric Lindros suffered as a Philadelphia Flyer?

A. Between two and three years
B. Between three and four years
C. Between four and five years
D. Between five and six years

4.10 What is the shortest NHL career for a NHL penalty leader?

A. 18 games
B. 38 games
C. 68 games
D. 98 games

4.11 Since the 70-game NHL schedule was introduced in 1949–50, what is the lowest penalty-minute total for a penalty leader in one season?

A. Fewer than 130 minutes
B. Between 130 and 160 minutes
C. Between 160 and 190 minutes
D. More than 190 minutes

4.12 Among NHLers with 2,000 penalty minutes or more, as of 2000–01 who has the most penalty minutes per goals scored in a career?

A. Ken Baumgartner
B. Shane Churla
C. Rob Ray
D. Kelly Chase

4.13 How much money did Brad May forfeit after being suspended for 20 games for slashing Steve Heinze in November 2000?

A. US$50,000 to $100,000

B. US$100,000 to $150,000

C. US$150,000 to $200,000

D. More than US$200,000

4.14 As of 2000–01, which 500-goal scorer has the most career penalty minutes?

A. Dino Ciccarelli

B. Stan Mikita

C. Bryan Trottier

D. Pat Verbeek

4.15 What is the least amount of points scored by an NHL penalty leader during his league-high penalty year?

A. Zero points

B. One point

C. Four points

D. Nine points

4.16 What is greatest span of time between penalty-leading years (the first and last years) for an NHL penalty leader?

A. Five years

B. Seven years

C. Nine years

D. 11 years

4.17 Which is the only NHL team since 1967 expansion to have two different penalty leaders in consecutive years?

A. The Pittsburgh Penguins

B. The Vancouver Canucks

C. The Buffalo Sabres

D. The Philadelphia Flyers

4.18 What is the longest suspension handed out during the playoffs?
A. Six games
B. 11 games
C. 16 games
D. 21 games

4.19 Of all the players to win the Rookie of the Year award, who amassed the most penalty minutes?
A. Bobby Orr
B. Denis Potvin
C. Willi Plett
D. Gary Suter

4.20 What tough guy helped New York capture its first Stanley Cup in 54 years in 1994 and later helped Detroit break a 42-year drought when they won the Cup in 1997?
A. Mike Peluso
B. Jay Wells
C. Joey Kocur
D. Kirk Maltby

PRINCES OF PAIN
Answers

4.1 C. 23 games
As of 2000–01, two players have earned league-leading 23-game suspensions, Marty McSorley and Gordie Dwyer. McSorley, the third-most penalized player in NHL history, was assessed 23 games—the number of games remaining in 1999–2000—after cracking Donald Brashear across the noggin on February 21, 2000. Dwyer, in a pre-season match-up between Tampa Bay and Washington on September 19, 2000, was handed 23 games after applying force to linesman David Brisebois in a scuffle with two Capitals. Dwyer then exited the penalty box and pulled referee Mark Faucette to the ice. Each incident drew an automatic sus-

pension totaling 23 games. It could be argued that McSorley ultimately received the longer suspension. After later meeting with NHL officials, McSorley's 23-game sentence was jacked up to a full year off the ice, or the equivalent of an 82-game season.

4.2   B. Tony Twist

It might have been Tony Twist's toughest fight. Unfortunately after being awarded US$24.5 million by a St. Louis jury in a court battle over a comic and animated series featuring a vulgar mobster named Antonio Twistelli (and nicknamed Tony Twist), a judge on appeal tossed out the July 2000 decision, disputing the lower court's ruling that it hindered Twist's endorsement possibilities. But Twist, who collected only 10 goals and piled up 1,121 penalty minutes in 10 NHL seasons, didn't leave without bloodying his opponent. He earlier settled for US$5 million out of court with HBO.

4.3   A. Donald Brashear

No fines or disciplinary action were levied, but Vancouver's Donald Brashear received notice from the league to stop his hand-wiping taunts after officials saw videos of the tough guy wiping his hands following an October 12, 2000, dust-up with Greg de Vries of Colorado. Buffalo Sabres tough guy Rob Ray admitted "We've all done it, we're all guilty of it," but said Brashear's timing couldn't be worse. "Right now Brash is the last guy who should be doing that," said Ray, referring to recent testimony from Marty McSorley that taunting contributed to his stick-swinging assault on Brashear in February 2000. When league officials called Canuck general manager Brian Burke with a request that Brashear stop it, Burke said: "I told them until there's a rule prohibiting it, don't bug my guy." In the NFL there is a rule banning all throat-slashing gestures.

4.4   A. Pat Egan

Scrappy defender Pat Egan played on four NHL clubs in 11 years during the 1940s and early 1950s. He earned his tough-guy reputation and the nickname Box-Car in 1941–42 when he accumulated a league-high 124 minutes in box time. In subsequent years he was usually among the top penalty leaders to lay on the lumber, including 1944–45 when he won the penalty crown again accumulating 86 minutes. Box-Car quit the NHL with 776 penalty minutes in 554 games.

4.5 D. More than 200 stitches
There is no definitive proof, but the NHL record for most stitches to close a facial wound in an on-ice incident probably belongs to Toronto's Borje Salming, who required more than 200 stitches in his face after being accidentally cut by the skate of Detroit winger Gerard Gallant on November 26, 1986. Salming's gash extended from his mouth, snaked up his right cheek to the inside of his right eye and up over his brow. The Leaf defenseman was lost to Toronto for 24 games in 1986–87.

4.6 D. Dave Williams
Dave "Tiger" Williams did more than just rack up box time pummeling players; he scored with relative consistency, beating every other NHL penalty leader in most goals in a PIM-leading season, including the great Maurice Richard, one the league's toughest

---

MOST GOALS SCORED IN A SEASON BY A PENALTY LEADER

Player	Season	GP	Goals	Points	PIM
Dave Williams	1980-81	77	35	62	343
Bob Probert	1987-88	74	29	62	398
Joe Lamb	1929-30	44	29	49	119
Maurice Richard	1952-53	70	28	61	112
Billy Boucher	1922-23	24	24	31	55
Ted Lindsay	1958-59	70	22	58	184

Current to 2000–01

players of all time. In 1980–81 Williams scored 35 goals and 62 points with a league-leading 343 penalty minutes. Bob Probert scored 29 goals but tied Williams in point totals (62) in 1987–88 and Richard had 28 goals for 61 points in 1952–53. While Richard, Probert and Williams all played in 70 or more games to accumulate their goal totals, little-known Joe Lamb of the Ottawa Senators, scored 29 goals in the 44-game 1929–30 season.

4.7 A. 43 goals
Chris Simon's extraordinary transition from brawler to first-line forward was the talk of 1999–2000. Washington's comeback kid had a career year, notching 29 goals, just 14 fewer than his entire output of seven previous seasons, 43 goals. What changed? Simon improved his skating and the release of his shot, which earned him more ice time. He also stayed healthy to play 75 games and record 201 shots, almost double the number of shots in his last best season, 1995–96's 105-shot year. His reputation for toughness is another factor that helped his goal surge; it precedes him into every corner in every NHL arena. Unfortunately, the numbers weren't on the board for Simon in 2000–01. In a story straight out of the bible's Samson and Delilah, Simon cut his long, legendary mane and, like Samson, lost his power. He fell below the 20-goal mark in 2000–01.

4.8 B. Scott Stevens
As of 2000–01, Eric Lindros suffered six concussions, his sixth coming on a thundering hit from New Jersey's Scott Stevens during the 2000 playoffs. Lindros, with his head down, was cutting across the Devils' offensive blueline when Stevens steamed across the rink and put the full force of his shoulder into the Flyer superstar. The hit was clean but Stevens remained unnerved by his blow to Lindros: "I'm just trying to put the (hit) behind me. I don't want to talk about it," Stevens said shortly after. The play rivetted the hockey world, set the Flyers on their heels during the series and put Lindros' future in doubt. When asked about

Stevens a few days later, Lindros said: "Leave the guy alone. He was doing his job." Would Stevens do the same thing again given the circumstances? Stevens told the *New York Post:* "It depends on what time of year it would be. I mean, in the playoffs everything is at stake. So no matter what my personal feelings are, my obligation to myself and my teammates is to play to win."

4.9   **A. Between two and three years**
Eric Lindros suffered six concussions between March 7, 1998 and May 26, 2000, a 27-month period that saw his status fall as arguably hockey's best player to its most fragile; and, ultimately, its most unbankable.

THE ERIC LINDROS CONCUSSIONS 1992–2000

Date	Hit	Games Lost
3.7.1998	Hit on chin by Pittsburgh's Darius Kasparaitis	18 games
12.27.1999	Hit by Jason Wiemer of the Calgary Flames	2 games
1.14.2000	Hit twice on the same shift by Chris Tamer in Atlanta	4 games
3.14.2000	Hit by Boston defenseman Hal Gill. Played three games and removed himself from lineup, missing the remainder of regular season.	
5.04.2000	Collided with Francis Lessard of the Philadelphia Phantoms while practising with the Flyer farm team.	
5.26.2000	Playing in just his second game since March, Lindros is flattened by New Jersey's Scott Stevens.	

4.10 B. 38 games

The shortest NHL career for a penalty leader belongs to Montreal Canadiens old-timer Joe Hall, the two-time penalty king from the league's first two seasons in 1917–18 and 1918–19. Hall played only 38 games over the two 24-game schedules. He then retired, having spent a long career in numerous pro leagues, including the forerunner to the NHL, the NHA, where he played defense for the Quebec Bulldogs for eight years, two producing Stanley Cup championships. In more modern times Montreal's Mike McMahon had the next shortest NHL career among penalty leaders. A defenseman with the Quebec Aces in the Quebec Senior Hockey League, McMahon joined the Canadiens in 1943–44, amassed a league-leading 98 minutes (and 24 points) in the 50-game schedule and helped Montreal win its first Stanley Cup in 13 years. In the playoffs he matched his defensive partners in points with three in eight games while collecting the second most penalty minutes (16) in the postseason. Parachuted into the NHL's top team, things couldn't be better for the 5-foot-8, 215-pound McMahon. He even stood next to Maurice Richard in the team photo for the Stanley Cup. But the following season he was demoted to the Montreal Royals of the QSHL. McMahon managed only another 15 NHL games (split between Montreal and Boston in 1945–46) before spending his remaining years in the minors. McMahon's 57-game career is the briefest among modern-day NHL penalty leaders.

4.11 A. Fewer than 130 minutes

In 1952–53 Maurice Richard topped the league with 112 penalty minutes, the lowest total for a penalty leader in the last 50 years. Despite his offensive skills, Richard was one of the NHL's most frequently penalized players. With no team policeman to protect him, he had to defend himself against the league's roughest players. During his career as hockey's best player, he racked up a hefty 1,285 penalty minutes. In 1953–54, when he led the league with 37 goals, he finished with 112 penalty minutes, just 20 minutes fewer than Gus Mortson's league-high 132-minute total.

4.12 **A. Ken Baumgartner**

Among the 41 NHLers with 2,000 penalty minutes or more as of 2000–01, there are players of varying offensive skill levels, ranging from 500-goal scorers to those with less than 20 goals in a career. Ken Baumgartner was no 500-goal scorer, but he did bring more than muscle to the game. Coupled with his willingness to fight was a no-holds-barred hockey enthusiasm that won him a regular position on five teams and made him a fan favourite they called "The Bomber." With just 13 career goals Baumgartner averaged only one red light per year but accumulated 2,244 minutes in box time, a ratio of 173 penalty minutes per goals scored, the best (or worst) in this category. Bryan Watson with 17 goals and 2,212 minutes ranks second at 130 minutes per goal; Mick Vukota, third with 17 goals and 2,017 minutes for 122 minutes per goal; and Kelly Chase, fourth with 17 goals and 2,017 for 118 minutes per goal. Among those with 1,000 PIM or more the ratios jump dramatically. Our best example is Randy Holt who scored just four goals but piled up 1,438 penalty minutes. That's a mind-boggling ratio of 360 PIM per goal (or six games in the penalty box for every goal scored).

4.13 **B. US$100,000 to $150,000**

Phoenix's Brad May lost US$117,647.05 in salary after receiving the fourth longest suspension in NHL history in November 2000. May's suspension for bashing Steve Heinze with a baseball-style swing across the face came shortly after Marty McSorley's year-long suspension for clubbing Donald Brashear in February 2000. May, then Brashear's Vancouver teammate, responded at the time to McSorley's hit by saying: "I have no respect for that guy ever again." Heinze was McSorley's teammate in Boston at the time of the Brashear attack. Was it a settling of accounts between tough guys? "I hope the McSorley incident had nothing to do with this," said Phoenix general manager Bobby Smith. May, known for his rugged play, had never been suspended before. He later apologized to Heinze, who needed nine stitches to close the gash.

On the ensuing power play Heinze got a little payback of his own. He scored and was later named the game's first star.

4.14 D. Pat Verbeek

The only 500-goal scorer to collect more than 2,000 penalty minutes is Pat Verbeek, a character player built with that rare mix of part pitbull and part sniper. While amassing the ninth highest penalty total in NHL history (2,760 minutes and counting), Verbeek was potting goals, mostly from in tight. His tenacity around the net during 18 seasons earned him his 500th in his 1,285th game on March 22, 2000. Only one other player took longer to reach that honoured plateau, Johnny Bucyk (who will likely be usurped in this category by Ron Francis in 2001–02).

4.15 B. One point

No NHL penalty leader has ever gone scoreless during the year he led the league in penalties, but Detroit defenseman Harvey "Hard Rock" Rockburn came within a single assist after a 0–1–1 season in 1930–31. Hard Rock, one of only three NHL regulars to score one point that year, sat in the box for a league-best 118 penalty minutes. Among today's penalty leaders no one can top Buffalo bad boy Rob Ray. Despite no appreciable hockey skills at the NHL level, Ray has carved out an NHL career as arguably the league's number one fighter, scoring under 40 goals in 12 seasons. As penalty leader in 1998–99, Ray established a modern-day low of just four points (all assists) in 76 games.

4.16 D. 11 years

In today's game Buffalo's Rob Ray has the most years between penalty-leading seasons: eight years from his first in 1990–91 (350 minutes) to his latest in 1998–99 (261 minutes). But no NHL tough guy to date can touch old-timer Gus Mortson, who led the league in penalty minutes four times, his first in his rookie year, 1946–47 (133 minutes) and his last in 1956–57 (147 minutes), 11 seasons later. He was a good skater and effective rusher, but his aggressive play as one of the era's hardest-hitting defenseman produced big box time, mostly for charging and boarding, but also for fighting. On at least one occasion he was fined and suspended for attempting to injure. Mortson, 32 years old in his last penalty-leading season, 1956–57, was one of the oldest penalty leaders in NHL history.

4.17 B. The Vancouver Canucks
Since expansion in 1967 Vancouver is the only team with different penalty leaders in back-to-back years. With former NHL tough guy Pat Quinn as general manager, the Canucks iced Gino Odjick and Donald Brashear, penalty leaders in 1996–97 and 1997–98. Odjick collected 371 penalty minutes and Brashear, who wanted to break Odjick's team record, did it by one minute, 372.

4.18 D. 21 games
Washington's Dale Hunter was handed a 21-game suspension for hitting Pierre Turgeon into the boards after the Islander forward scored a game-winning and series-winning goal on April 28, 1993. It is the second longest player-on-player suspension in NHL history after Marty McSorley's 23-game/one-year ban in February 2000.

4.19 B. Denis Potvin
In his 15-year Hall of Fame career defenseman Denis Potvin never had more penalty minutes in one year than in his rookie season, 1973–74, when he amassed a record 175 minutes, tops among all Calder winners in NHL history. The New York Islanders' first overall pick of 1973 proved, as he did in five previous seasons with the OHA Ottawa 67s, that his game-play was equal at both ends of the ice, racking up his 175-minute penalty count while scoring 54 points in 74 games as a rookie blueliner. Not surprisingly, all penalty leaders among Calder winners are defensemen.

ROOKIE OF THE YEAR PENALTY LEADERS

Player	Team	Year	G-A-Pts	PIM
Denis Potvin	NYI	1973-74	17-37-54	175
Gary Suter	Calgary	1985-86	18-50-68	141
Willi Plett	Atlanta	1976-77	33-23-56	123
Kent Douglas	Toronto	1962-63	7-15-22	105
Jacques Laperriere	Montreal	1963-64	2-28-30	102
Bobby Orr	Boston	1966-67	13-28-41	102

Current to 2000–01

4.20 C. Joey Kocur

Every team needs a scrapper with a head on his shoulders come playoff time and Joey Kocur fit the bill perfectly during the 1990s. With Kocur in the line-ups of New York and Detroit—the two NHL teams with the league's longest Cup-less streaks—the Rangers snapped 54 years of frustration with their 1994 Cup victory and later, in 1997 and 1998, the Red Wings won championships after a 42-year drought. Kocur is one of a very few NHLers who claimed as many as three Stanley Cups during the 1990s. (Larry Murphy had four in the decade.)

Game 4

HOCKEY CROSSWORD

(Solutions are on page 121)

ACROSS

1. _____ Jagr
5. Alexei _____
8. _____ Oilers
10. _____ Kariya
11. Toronto's Darcy _____
12. New Jersey's Jason _____
14. The Rangers' Valeri _____
15. Florida rookie _____ Novoseltsev
16. Opposite of loser
19. Ranger goalie Mike _____
20. _____ -Star Game
21. Defenseman Sean _____
23. Best old Russian unit: The _____ Line (abbrv.)
26. Goalie Jacques _____
28. Tough guy _____ May
29. Boston's Joe _____
31. Old-time goalie Harry _____

DOWN

1. Colorado star (full name)
2. Oiler-Isles D-man from Czech Republic (full name)
3. Too many _____ on the ice
4. The Maurice Richard _____
5. New _____ Rangers
6. Calgary 1st choice in 1999, Oleg _____
7. Tampa Bay-Chicago centre: Michael _____ of Sweden
9. Phoenix's Teppo _____ of Finland
13. Keith _____ of the Coyotes
17. Calgary's Jarome _____
18. San Jose's Owen _____
20. Chicago sniper Tony _____
22. Theoren _____
24. Three-time Edmonton Cup-winner, Craig _____
25. Columbus winger Robert _____
26. Public relations (abbrv.)
27. _____ Oates
30. Extra period (abbrv.)

5
TRUE OR FALSE?

Has any former NHL goalkeeper ever coached a team to a Stanley Cup championship? In this chapter we give you a 50–50 chance of scoring a right answer with some true or false questions. In this case, it's true. NHL goalkeepers haven't had much luck behind the bench. No ex-goalie has ever coached a Stanley Cup winner, and only one former netminder has ever coached in a Cup finals: Emile Francis, whose New York Rangers lost to the Boston Bruins in the 1972 showdown.

(*Answers are on page 68*)

5.1 When Mario Lemieux returned from retirement in 2000–01, he wore the Penguins captain's "C". **True or False?**

5.2 All six team captains of Canadian NHL clubs at the start of 2000–01 were born outside of Canada. **True or False?**

5.3 John LeClair is the only U.S.-born player to net three 50-goal seasons. **True or False?**

5.4 St. Louis' Chris Pronger is the youngest Hart Trophy winner (league MVP) among defenseman in NHL history. **True or False?**

5.5 Columbus winger Steve Heinze wore No. 57 with the Blue Jackets in 2000–01. **True or False?**

5.6 NHL players traditionally receive a silver stick after scoring their 1,000th point. **True or False?**

5.7 Since joining the NHL in its inaugural season, Toronto has had three different names: the Arenas (1917–18 to 1918–19), the

St. Patricks (1919–20 to 1925–26) and the Maple Leafs (1926–27 to present day). No player has ever worn the jerseys for all of Toronto's NHL teams. **True or False?**

5.8 As of 1999–2000, no European goalie has led his team to the Stanley Cup. **True or False?**

5.9 Fighter Rob Ray has never won an individual NHL award. **True or False?**

5.10 Hockey players with vision in only one eye are ineligible to play hockey in the NHL. **True or False?**

5.11 The first goaltender to don a mask during play was actually a woman. **True or False?**

5.12 Soviet goalie great Valdislav Tretiak is the first European-trained player in the Hockey Hall of Fame. **True or False?**

5.13 Ken Morrow of the New York Islanders is the only member of the 1980 gold medal-winning U.S. Olympic team to win the Stanley Cup. **True or False?**

5.14 Mark Messier never led the Vancouver Canucks to the playoffs. **True or False?**

5.15 Maurice Richard, Bobby Orr and Mario Lemieux all recorded their best point performance when they were 23 years old. **True or False?**

5.16 Colorado star forwards Chris Drury and Milan Hejduk were actually selected by the Quebec Nordiques during that team's last draft year before the Nordiques were transferred to Denver in 1995. **True or False?**

5.17 Wayne Gretzky scored more points in his first NHL season than any other rookie in history. **True or False?**

5.18 Bobby Orr ranked among the NHL's top 10 scorers in more seasons than any other defenseman in history. **True or False?**

5.19 When New Jersey Devils captain Scott Stevens won the Conn Smythe Trophy as MVP of the 2000 Stanley Cup playoffs, he joined Bobby Orr as only the second defenseman to claim the coveted award. **True or False?**

5.20 Grace and Louis Sutter, parents of the six NHL-playing Sutter brothers, actually had seven sons. **True or False?**

5.21 After the death of hockey's most famous No. 9, Maurice Richard, in 2000, teams representing Quebec in national competition were no longer allowed to use No. 9. **True or False?**

5.22 Since Montreal's Tom Johnson and Doug Harvey won Norris Trophies (top defenseman) in 1959 and 1960 respectively, no other team has had back-to-back winners. **True or False?**

5.23 After goalie Pelle Lindbergh died in 1985, no Philadelphia Flyer has worn his No. 31. **True or False?**

5.24 Scotty Bowman's career victories exceed the total number of NHL games coached by any other individual. **True or False?**

5.25 The historic puck that Paul Henderson shot past Vladislav Tretiak in Moscow to win the 1972 Summit Series between Team Canada and the Soviet Union is in the Hockey Hall of Fame. **True or False?**

5.26 In 2000–01, both Petr Svobodas, the 20-year-old rookie with Toronto and the 34-year-old veteran with Tampa Bay, wore No. 23 on their jerseys. **True or False?**

5.27 No two top overall picks from one NHL draft year have come from American universities. **True or False?**

5.28 No player in NHL history who has scored a five-goal game did so in a losing cause. **True or False?**

5.29 Only one Calder Trophy winner (rookie of the year), Bobby Orr, scored a Stanley Cup-winning goal in his career. **True or False?**

5.30 Legendary old-time goaltender Terry Sawchuk publicly insisted he wouldn't wear a goalie mask. **True or False?**

5.31 Only one player, the great Toe Blake, played for both the Montreal Maroons and the Montreal Canadiens. **True or False?**

5.32 Before Detroit became the Red Wings they were known as the Falcons and the Cougars during the 1920s and early 1930s. No player has ever played for Detroit under all three team names. **True or False?**

5.33 Before Denny Lambert recorded an NHL-high 219 penalty minutes for the Atlanta Thrashers in their inaugural season 1999–2000, no player in league history had ever lead the league in penalty minutes for an expansion team in its first year. **True or False?**

5.34 No NHLer has ever led the league in penalty minutes in back-to-back years with different teams. **True or False?**

5.35 The first NHL team to win its first two playoff games was the Los Angeles Kings. **True or False?**

5.36 Jeremy Roenick never played a game in the minors. **True or False?**

5.37 Besides old-timer Carl Voss, no NHL rookie of the year was ever traded mid-season during his Calder-winning season. **True or False?**

5.38 When tough guy Gino Odjick was obtained by the Montreal Canadiens in December 2000, he was given Hall of Famer Ken Dryden's old sweater number, No. 29. **True or False?**

5.39 During the six-team era between 1942–43 and 1966–67 no fourth-place team ever won the Stanley Cup. **True or False?**

5.40 Each time the Pittsburgh Penguins won the Stanley Cup in 1990–91 and 1991–92, they finished with exactly the same point-spread behind the regular-season league leaders, 18 points. **True or False?**

TRUE OR FALSE?
Answers

5.1 **False.** As CEO of the Penguins, Mario Lemieux could have asked for the "C" but instead insisted that Jaromir Jagr remain Pittsburgh's captain. Jagr, mired in a slump at the time of Mario's return, said: "It's not a big problem who's going to be captain. He's been the man for so long, and will always be the man. Whatever he wants me to do, I'll do. I respect him so much."

5.2 **True.** Markus Naslund (Vancouver), Daniel Alfredsson (Ottawa) and Mats Sundin (Toronto) are from Sweden; Saku Koivu (Montreal) is from Finland; Doug Weight (Edmonton) is American; and Steve Smith (Calgary) is Canadian-raised but born in Scotland.

5.3   **True.** John LeClair from St. Albans, Vermont is the first and only American-born NHLer to record three 50-goal seasons and three consecutive 50-goal seasons, 1995–96 (51), 1996–97 (50) and 1997–98 (51). Brett Hull, who has five 50-goal years and plays for the U.S. Team in international competition, is a Canadian by birth from Belleville, Ontario.

5.4   **False.** Pronger, 25 years old in 2000 when he won his Hart, is the second youngest defenseman among only five rearguards named MVP in NHL history. Bobby Orr won MVP status at 23 in 1970.

5.5   **True.** Before Columbus selected Steve Heinze at the NHL Expansion Draft in 2000, the Boston right winger wore No. 23. When his nine-year career with the Bruins ended, Heinze chose No. 57, the number made famous by the popular food manufacturer of the same name.

5.6   **True.** Traditionally players who hit the 1,000-point milestone receive a silver stick from their team, except in the case of Washington's Joe Reekie, the Caps' low-scoring defenseman, who was given a mock silver stick by teammates after snapping a 198-game slump with a goal on December 2, 2000, against Boston. Reekie went scoreless through the second half of 1997–98, all of 1998–99 and 1999–2000 and the first 22 games of 2000–01.

5.7   **False.** Our research found just one player, centre Corb Denneny, who played with Toronto's three NHL teams—the Arenas, the St. Pats and the Maple Leafs—during his career. Denneny suited up for the Arenas in two NHL seasons (1917–18 and 1918–19) and then four seasons with the St. Pats (1919–20 to 1922–23), winning Stanley Cups with each club. He later joined the Maple Leafs for their inaugural season, 1926–27. But Denneny's connection to Toronto doesn't end there. He also played for the Toronto Shamrocks and the Toronto Blueshirts of the NHA, the predecessor to the NHL.

Denneny has worn more Toronto sweaters on more pro teams in Toronto than any other player.

5.8 **True.** Despite the emergence of many great Euro netminders in the NHL, none has led his club to a Stanley Cup. Canadian and American goalies still dominate the winner's circle, but it's only a matter of time before a Dominik Hasek or Roman Turek captures the championship. As New York Ranger broadcaster and former NHL goalie John Davidson pointed out in *Ultimate Sports Hockey*: "I think it was difficult for European goaltenders because the angles are different on the wider (European) surfaces."

5.9 **False.** During his 11-plus seasons with Buffalo, pugilist Rob Ray has earned his place in the NHL almost entirely with his fists. Away from the ice Ray fights his battles against illness and disease, spending much of his free time helping numerous charitable organizations such as March of Dimes, Make-a-Wish Foundation, Children's Hospital, Walk America and Roswell Park Cancer Institute. His commitment to the community in 1999 won Ray the NHL's King Clancy Memorial Trophy, awarded to the "player who best exemplifies leadership qualities on and off the ice and has made a noteworthy humanitarian contribution to his community."

5.10 **True.** Under NHL by-laws, a player with one eye or less than 3/60th vision in one eye, is ineligible to play. This is not the case in the AHL where there are no regulations prohibiting partially sighted players from taking a regular shift.

5.11 **True.** Decades before Jacques Plante became hockey's first goalie to regularly wear a mask and three years before Clint Benedict tried a crude leather face mask for a few games in 1930, Queen's University goalie Elizabeth Graham wore a wire fencing mask during intercollegiate games beginning in 1927. The *Montreal Star* reported: "The Queen's goalie gave the fans a surprise when she stepped into the nets and then donned a fencing mask. It was safety first with her and even at that she can't be blamed for her precautionary methods."

5.12 **True.** Vladislav Tretiak came to prominence after stoning Canada's best at the historic 1972 Summit Series. Considered one of the finest goaltenders in the history of hockey, Tretiak won three Olympic gold medals, one Canada Cup and 10 World Championships between 1970 and 1984. Swedish defenseman Borje Salming and Peter Stastny of Czechoslovakia are also enshrined in the Hall.

5.13 **False.** Besides Ken Morrow, who won four consecutive Stanley Cups with the Islanders between 1980 and 1983, the only other player from the 1980 Olympic gold medal American team to win the Cup is Neal Broten, champion with the New Jersey Devils in 1995.

5.14 **True.** Despite a contract that paid him US$6 million annually, Mark Messier never scored more than 22 goals during his three seasons for Vancouver and never led the Canucks into postseason play.

5.15 **False.** Bobby Orr and Mario Lemieux each scored the most points in their careers at age 23 (Orr in 1970–71 with 139 points and Lemieux in 1988–89 with 199 points); but while Richard recorded his best goal season at age 23 (50 goals in 1944–45) his top point output was in 1954–55 when he bested his 73-point effort of 1944–45 by just one point with 74 in 1954–55. He was 33 years old.

5.16 **True.** Two of Colorado's brightest prospects were drafted in 1994 when Nordiques rookie general manager Pierre LaCroix plucked Chris Drury and Milan Hejduk deep in the draft. Drury, an American from Boston University, was chosen 72nd overall, and Hejduk, from the Czech Republic, went 87th. Four short years later, Lacroix's "Nordiques picks" turned into the Avalanche's future, as Drury won 1998-99's rookie of the year honours and Hejduk notched 48 points, four more than Drury's 44 that season.

5.17 **True.** Wayne Gretzky collected 137 points on 51 goals and 86 assists in his freshman NHL season in 1979–80. That's five points more than Teemu Selanne bagged in his remarkable first year with the Winnipeg Jets in 1992–93. However, Selanne, not Gretzky, holds the NHL rookie record. Gretzky, only 19 at the time, did not qualify as a true rookie because he had played the previous year in the rival World Hockey Association.

5.18 **False.** Defenseman Paul Coffey placed among the top-10 scorers six times in his NHL career, which equals Bobby Orr's mark for most by a rearguard. Coffey earned his sixth top-10 finish during the lockout-shortened 1994–95 season, while patrolling the blueline for the Detroit Red Wings. Coffey also made the grade twice with the Pittsburgh Penguins and three times with the Edmonton Oilers. Orr finished among the league's top 10 six straight seasons with the Boston Bruins from 1970 to 1975. During that span, Orr captured two scoring titles and never ranked lower than third.

5.19 **False.** Scott Stevens was actually the sixth defenseman to win the Conn Smythe Trophy. The other blueliners to claim the hardware were Serge Savard (1969), Bobby Orr (1970 and 1972), Larry Robinson (1978), Al MacInnis (1989) and Brian Leetch (1994).

5.20 **True.** The six Sutter brothers—Brian, Duane, Darryl, Brent, Rick and Ron—had another brother, Gary, who never played hockey but as Brent said: "Gary would have made it because when we were young, he was the best of all of us."

5.21 **True.** In August 2000, Hockey Quebec, the association that handles the province's minor-hockey development program, announced that teams representing Quebec in national competition cannot use No. 9—the number worn by French Canada's greatest hockey player, the late Maurice Richard. Hockey Quebec represents 90,000 young players.

5.22 **False.** A number of teams have iced defensemen (Paul Coffey, Ray Bourque, Rod Langway) with consecutive Norris Trophies, but no club can claim back-to-back Norrises by two players with the exception of Montreal and St. Louis. Exactly 40 years after Tom Johnson (1959) and Doug Harvey (1960) won their Norrises with the Canadiens, St. Louis became just the second team with Norris teammates in consecutive years, Al MacInnis in 1999 and Chris Pronger in 2000.

5.23 **True.** Even though Pelle Lindbergh's No. 31 is still active (it has never been officially retired to the rafters of First Union Center), Philadelphia has never assigned his jersey number to any other player. Lindbergh, the reigning Vezina Trophy winner as the NHL's top goalie, died on November 10, 1985 after crashing his Porsche 930 Turbo at a very high speed. The Flyer goalie had a blood-alcohol level of .24, a figure considerably higher than the .10 legal limit. He was 26 years old. On the 15th anniversary of Pelle's death, Flyer equipment manager Jim Evers said in the *Philadelphia Daily News:* "One guy, Neil Little, asked for it (Lindbergh's sweater number) when he first got here. He didn't know, and he was OK with it when I explained it to him."

5.24 **False.** To put Scotty Bowman's amazing career totals in perspective, his 1,157 career wins alone (in mid-2000–01) surpass the game-coached totals of all but two bench bosses: Al Arbour's 1,606 and Dick Irvin's 1,449. Only five other men in league annals have coached 1,000 career games.

5.25 **False.** There's no logo or other identifying characteristic on it, but somewhere out there is hockey's most prized puck. The black circular rubber disc that Paul Henderson used to score the series-winning goal in 1972's famous Summit Series is not preserved under glass in the Hockey Hall of Fame but possibly lost, the whereabouts known to maybe only three men: Henderson and teammates Pat Stapleton and Bill White. Video of the celebrated goal shows Henderson being embraced by teammates as Stapleton retrieves the puck. In a November 2000 Canadian Press story, Henderson maintains he doesn't have it but would like in the Hall of Fame. Stapleton and White each claim it's in the other's possession. "I always tell people I gave it to Bill White, and they can bother him," Stapleton said. "He's just trying to throw everybody off the trail," White countered, believing that Stapleton has it hidden in a safety deposit box. Why all the secrecy? "Once we disclose where it is, the mystery is gone and I've got nothing to talk about," said Stapleton. For Henderson, the man who scored the goal, it's a question of finders-keepers: "He (Stapleton) had the foresight to pick it up and see the value in it later on down the road...Patty has it and it's his prerogative to do what he wants with it."

5.26 **True.** Besides each playing defense, the two Czech-born Petr Svobodas have little else in common, except their sweater numbers, No. 23.

5.27 **False.** The first time two teams picked American college boys No. 1 and No. 2 in the NHL Entry Draft was in 2000 when goalie Rick DiPietro of Boston University went first overall to the New York Islanders and then the expansion Atlanta Thrashers selected University of Wisconsin winger Dany Heatley second.

5.28 **True.** No NHLer has ever scored five times in a game and lost, but Winnipeg's Alexei Zhamnov's five-goal performance on April 1, 1995, was almost wasted (or seemed like a very bad April Fool's joke) as his Jets couldn't stem Los Angeles' attack in the 7–7 knot. Kelly Hrudey (3) and Grant Fuhr (2) of the Kings shared the blame in Zhamnov's five-goal output.

CALDER TROPHY–STANLEY CUP GOAL SCORERS

Rookie	Calder Trophy	Stanley Cup Goal
Carl Voss	1933/Detroit	1938/Chicago
Bernie Geoffrion	1952/Montreal	1958/Montreal
Bobby Orr	1967/Boston	1970, 1972/Boston
Mike Bossy	1978/Islanders	1982, 1983/Isles
Bobby Smith	1979/Minnesota	1986/Montreal

Current to 2000

5.29 **False.** Since 1933 when the first Calder Trophy was awarded to Carl Voss, only five rookie award winners have scored Stanley Cup-winning goals. Top rookies Bobby Orr and Mike Bossy each scored multiple Cup-winners.

5.30 **True.** When Montreal goalie Jacques Plante became the NHL's first masked goalie in 1959, he faced many detractors, including members of his own fraternity such as Terry Sawchuk, who didn't exactly embrace the idea. "Just because Jacques Plante wears a mask, some people figure that makes a big difference," said Sawchuk. "I've been a pro goalie for more than a dozen years and I've never worn a mask in a game. I don't see any reason for starting now." Three years after Plante (and the introduction of the slapshot), Sawchuk slipped on a mask in 1962–63, becoming just the third NHL netminder to use face protection.

5.31 **False.** Besides Toe Blake at least 20 other players played for Montreal's two NHL teams, including Babe Siebert, Herb Cain and goalie Lorne Chabot. One of hockey's hottest old-time rivalries, the Canadiens and Maroons played 92 games against each other between 1924–25 and 1937–38, the Habs winning five games more during that 14-year stretch with a 40–35–17 record compared to the Maroons' 35–40–17. Each Montreal team won two Stanley Cups during that time.

5.32 **False.** Only four NHLers can say they played for all three Detroit teams in the NHL: Ebbie Goodfellow, Reg Noble, Larry Aurie and Herb Lewis. Before the winged wheel became synonymous with Detroit, the Red Wings were called the Cougars (1926–27 to 1929–30) and then the Falcons (1930–31 to 1931–32). Detroit struggled under both names until grain millionaire James Norris bought the franchise in 1932 and renamed the team Red Wings. Norris chose a logo similar to the emblem of the Montreal Amateur Athletic Association, a sporting club of which he was a member. The MAAA Winged Wheelers won the first Stanley Cup in 1893, and this was Norris' inspiration for his own NHL franchise. He kept longtime coach and general manager Jack Adams who had already begun assembling a nucleus of players of championship stature. Adams picked up Noble, Goodfellow, Aurie and Lewis in the late 1920s and each wore the sweaters of all three Detroit teams. Noble was sold to the Montreal Maroons for $7,500 after just five games as a Red Wing in 1932, but Goodfellow won three Stanley Cups and captained the team in the late 1930s and early 1940s before becoming a player-coach. Adams paired wingers Aurie and Lewis in 1928 and for the next 11 seasons they played on Detroit's first line, each becoming team scoring leader at least once. Aurie and Lewis were centered first by Cooney Weiland and later by Marty Barry. With Weiland, Aurie and Lewis's line averaged just 150 pounds, but their playmaking often outshone Toronto's famous Kid Line. In 1935 Adams stuck Barry between the two little wingers to give the unit more beef and Detroit won consecutive Stanley Cups in 1935–36 and 1936–37.

5.33 **False.** Since NHL expansion in 1967, it has happened two times: after an outstanding minor league career Barclay Plager joined first-year St. Louis in 1967 and amassed a league-best 153 penalty minutes; and in 1979–80 Jimmy Mann collected 287 minutes with the expansion Winnipeg Jets.

5.34 **True.** Only a few NHL penalty leaders have had successive league-high penalty totals (Keith Magnuson, Dave Schultz and Chris Nilan), but none have done it with two different teams in consecutive years.

5.35 **True.** No club in NHL history had won its first two playoff matches until Los Angeles beat Minnesota 2–1 (April 4) and 2–0 (April 6) during the 1968 Quarterfinals. Unfortunately, the Kings couldn't sustain their luck and bowed to the Stars in seven games.

5.36 **True.** After being selected eighth overall in the 1988 NHL Draft out of Thayer Academy, high-schooler Jeremy Roenick went right to the Chicago Blackhawks. His brief stopover in Hull with the Quebec Major Junior Hockey League's Olympiques proved he was NHL-ready. In 28 games with Hull, Roenick scored an incredible 70 points. When he was called up for Chicago's final 20 games he recorded 18 points.

5.37 **False.** Since 1933 there have been only two occasions when NHL teams traded away rookies in midseason who went on to win the Calder Trophy as the league's top freshman. Carl Voss, the very first Calder winner, was traded by New York for cash to Detroit in 1932 just 10 games (and three points) into the 1932–33 season. Voss scored 20 points in the next 38 games to win rookie of the year with the Red Wings. In 1954–55, Montreal literally gave away promising rookie Ed Litzenberger to shore up Chicago's faltering franchise. In 29 games with the sniper-rich Canadiens, Litzenberger scored just 11 points, but in Chicago as his ice time soared so did his point totals, collecting 40 points in 44 games to claim top rookie honours.

5.38 **True.** The Montreal Canadiens would probably have to retire 25 per cent of the team's sweater numbers between Jacques Plante's No. 1 and Patrick Roy's No. 33 to honour all the outstanding players who served hockey's most storied franchise. The once-proud club hit rock bottom several times in 2000–01, beginning with its slide to last place in league standings, the sale of the team (and the monstrous Molson Centre) to an American and the final insult to its glorious past: giving away Ken Dryden's No. 29 to bruiser journeyman Gino Odjick. Other prominent Canadiens numbers not retired include Bernie Geoffrion's No. 5, Dickie Moore and Yvan Cournoyer's No. 12, Serge Savard's No. 18, Larry Robinson's No. 19, Bob Gainey's No. 23, Jacques Lemaire's No. 25 and Ken Dryden's No. 29.

5.39 **False.** During the 25-year period of the NHL's six-team era only one club, the Toronto Maple Leafs, won the Stanley Cup after finishing the regular season in fourth place. Despite their status as two-time defending Stanley Cup champions, the Maple Leafs ended 1948–49 18 points back of first-place Detroit. But their fourth-place, 57-point regular season meant little in the playoffs as they defeated Boston in the semi-finals and then swept the Red Wings in four straight. With the championship Toronto became the first NHL club to win three consecutive Stanley Cups and nine straight victories in the finals (the first win dating back to April 19, 1947).

5.40 **True.** During their two Stanley Cup-winning seasons the Penguins finished exactly 18 points back of the NHL's first-place teams. In 1990–91 Pittsburgh had 88 points compared to first-place Chicago's 106-point finish; and in 1991–92 the Pens totalled 87 points, 18 less than the New York Rangers with 105.

Game 5
THE HIGH-FIVERS

Scoring five goals in a game is an extraordinary feat, so special that some NHL teams are still waiting for their first high-fiver. In this game match the high-five goal scorer with the club for whom he filled the net.

(*Solutions are on page 121*)

1. _____ Dave Andreychuk   A. Chicago Blackhawks

2. _____ Alexei Zhamnov   B. Toronto Maple Leafs

3. _____ Mats Sundin   C. Edmonton Oilers

4. _____ Joe Nieuwendyk   D. Buffalo Sabres

5. _____ John Tonelli   E. New York Rangers

6. _____ Ian Turnbull   F. Calgary Flames

7. _____ Tim Young   G. New York Islanders

8. _____ Pat Hughes   I. Quebec Nordiques

9. _____ Mark Pavelich   J. Winnipeg Jets

10. _____ Grant Mulvey   K. Minnesota North Stars

6
BANG FOR THE BUCK

After stepping down as longtime manager of the Boston Bruins in October 2000, Harry Sinden was asked whether, as president of the club, the Bruins would ever have a $10 million player. His reply: "Never. Seems to me it's pretty hard to put your face in front of a puck when you've got $40 million in the bank." In this chapter, we check out the biggest name in the game—money.

(Answers are on page 84)

6.1 In 2000–01 sweater manufacturers moved their trademark logos on NHL jerseys. Where are they now located on players' jerseys?
   A. Above the player nameplate
   B. On the right shoulder
   C. Below the team crest
   D. Below the player number

6.2 Which NHLer was recruited by Dallas Stars' owner Tom Hicks to court baseball's Alex Rodriguez before Rodriguez signed the richest contract in sports history with the Texas Rangers in December 2000?
   A. Wayne Gretzky
   B. Mike Modano
   C. Mario Lemieux
   D. Brett Hull

6.3 What item fetched the most money at the Maple Leaf Gardens' auction in November 2000?
   A. The Gardens' Zamboni
   B. The 1967 Stanley Cup Banner

C. The Gardens' home penalty box

D. The Gardens' nets

6.4 After being struck by an errant shot at Los Angeles' Great Western Forum in February 1999, how much money did hockey fan Jonathan Liebert receive in a settlement case?

A. US$3,000

B. US$30,000

C. US$300,000

D. US$3 million

6.5 What was NHLer John MacLean's salary after he cleared waivers and the New York Rangers sent him to the IHL Manitoba Moose?

A. US$2,500

B. US$25,000

C. US$250,000

D. US$2.5 million

6.6 On October 15, 2000, the player's model of Doug Harvey's James Norris Memorial Trophies (1955 to 1960) was put on the block at a Toronto auction house. What was the selling price of this authentic item?

A. $3,000

B. $5,000

C. $10,000

D. $15,000

6.7 Considering the average player salary topped US$1 million in 2000–01, what was the average salary when NHLPA executive director Bob Goodenow took over eight years earlier in 1992?

A. US$171,000 per season

B. US$271,000 per season

C. US$371,000 per season

D. US$471,000 per season

6.8 As of 2000–01 which player commanded the highest salary package in NHL history?
A. Jaromir Jagr
B. Mike Modano
C. Mario Lemieux
D. Paul Kariya

6.9 How much did Ottawa's Alexei Yashin forfeit in 1999–2000 by refusing to honour the final year of his contract?
A. US$2.6 million
B. US$3.6 million
C. US$4.6 million
D. US$5.6 million

6.10 When goalie Fred Brathwaite went to arbitration after his surprising 61-game performance for Calgary in 1999–2000, how much of a salary increase were the Flames ordered to pay Brathwaite in 2000–01?
A. A 53 per cent increase
B. A 103 per cent increase
C. A 153 per cent increase
D. A 203 per cent increase

6.11 Which player was awarded the most money in an arbitration case in NHL history?
A. Philadelphia's John LeClair
B. Calgary's Fred Brathwaite
C. Philadelphia's Mark Recchi
D. Phoenix's Keith Tkachuk

6.12 How much personal insurance did Eric Lindros have against injury in 2000–01, after suffering his near career-ending sixth concussion in 1999–2000?
A. None
B. US$5 million

C. US$10 million

D. US$20 million

6.13 How many Wayne Gretzky cards were being auctioned on eBay's Web site in 2000–01?

A. 215 cards

B. 515 cards

C. 915 cards

D. 1,215 cards

6.14 How much would Vancouver's Daniel or Henrik Sedin make in bonus money if either brother won the Calder Trophy as the NHL's top rookie in 2000–01?

A. US$400,000

B. US$600,000

C. US$800,000

D. US$1 million

6.15 Which NHL rookie made more money than any established star in the league upon signing his first contract?

A. Jean Beliveau

B. Bobby Orr

C. Wayne Gretzky

D. Paul Kariya

6.16 Considering that the average NHL player salary was US$1.4 million in 2000–01, what did the lowest paid NHLer make that year?

A. US$143,750

B. US$243,750

C. US$343,750

D. US$443,750

6.17 What was the combined payroll for NHL players in 2000–01?
A. US$500,000 million
B. US$700,000 million
C. US$900,000 million
D. More than US$1 billion

6.18 What was the average worth of an NHL franchise in 2000–01?
A. US$108 million
B. US$148 million
C. US$188 million
D. US$228 million

6.19 What NHL team has the highest average ticket prices in 2000–01?
A. The New York Rangers
B. The Colorado Avalanche
C. The Philadelphia Flyers
D. The Toronto Maple Leafs

BANG FOR THE BUCK
Answers

6.1 **A. Above the player nameplate**
In a five-year US$10 million deal, the NHL and The Hockey Company, which manufacturers Koho and CCM brands, agreed to relocate the trademarks from the bottom right of the back of the sweater to above the nameplate. Half of the 30 NHL teams will wear sweaters with the CCM logo, while the other 15 will wear Koho. The new logo placement improves the visibility of the only non-NHL corporate trademark allowed on NHL jerseys.

6.2 **B. Mike Modano**
To nab shortstop Alex Rodriguez, Dallas Stars and Texas Rangers' owner Tom Hicks asked the Stars' Mike Modano to show A-Rod

the sights of Dallas and join them in a dinner at Bob's Steak and Chop House. "I knew for sure he (Hicks) would be as aggressive as he is in his business dealings," Modano said. "Nobody ever thought that Brett Hull would sign with the Stars because of the style of game we played. But Mr. Hicks knew he (Hull) could help us win." The 25-year-old shortstop signed a 10-year, US$252 million contract with the Rangers, the richest in sports history.

6.3   B.   The 1967 Stanley Cup Banner
In the November 19, 2000, auction that stripped Maple Leaf Gardens down its bare concrete, everything that could be moved was sold off, including player banners, scoreboards, team benches, goal lights, penalty boxes, restroom signs and even the Zamboni. The priciest item was Toronto's 1967 Stanley Cup banner, which went to a telephone bidder for $60,000. The Zamboni sold for $26,000, a Leaf net got $10,500, the home penalty box brought $7,000 and George Armstrong's retired No. 10 banner earned $3,400. The most symbolic gesture of the day's proceedings was the sale of Conn Smythe's blue and white dressing room sign "Defeat does not rest lightly on their shoulders." It fetched $7,600.

6.4   D.   US$3 million
Fan Jonathan Liebert scored the biggest payoff of his life after successfully suing The Los Angeles Kings, the San Jose Sharks and ex-Shark winger Joe Murphy for $3 million after Murphy fired a puck out of frustration that hit Liebert in a game at the Great Western Forum on February 6, 1999. Liebert suffered post-concussion syndrome and claimed he lost the ability to work.

6.5   D.   US$2.5 million
It's an astronomical sum of money to pay someone for playing in the minors, but when 36-year-old John MacLean cleared waivers around the league in November 2000, New York general manager Glen Sather was forced to send the unhappy MacLean to the Rangers' IHL farm club, the Manitoba Moose. Sather had already

offered to pay 80 per cent (US$2 million) in trade talks, leaving other NHL teams to cough up just $500,000. Then, Sather tried to buy out MacLean at $2 million, but over two years. MacLean refused and his punishment was full salary (US$2.5 million) in the minors.

6.6   D. $15,000
Doug Harvey died a broke and broken man, but his eight-inch silver-plated trophy, awarded to the late Hall of Famer for five of his seven Norris Trophies, fetched $15,000 at an auction in October 2000. The dented and tarnished old trophy wasn't expected to go for more than $3,000. But the bidding, which was over in 90 seconds, went to an unknown tender for $15,000. Harvey originally gave the trophy to a Montreal restaurant owner. When the restauranteur tried to return it to Harvey, the all-star defenseman yelled "When I give a gift, I give a gift," hurling the award back at his friend. After hockey, Harvey's life declined into alcoholism and part-time jobs. His remaining days were spent in a renovated CN train car at an Ottawa-area race track. Harvey died of cirrhosis of the liver on Boxing Day, 1989.

6.7   B. US$271,000 per season
Under the tenure of Bob Goodenow, NHLers have experienced unprecedented salary growth. In eight short years, between 1992 and 2000, the average player wage has skyrocketed from US$271,000 to US$1.4 million. During the 1994–95 lockout-shortened season, when teams tried to rein in player costs the average salary was $733,000. It took only three years to get that average above $1 million. In 2000-01, the league average in team payroll was US$33 million. Goodenow played hockey at Harvard and was an Eastern College Athletic Conference all-star in 1974.

6.8   A. Jaromir Jagr
After MLB's Texas Rangers signed Alex Rodriguez to a 10-year, US$252 million deal in December 2000, the other three major

North American leagues compared notes. The highest salary package in basketball was the Minnesota Timberwolves' six-year, US$126 million deal with Kevin Garnett (1997–2002); the most expensive in football was the NFL's Dallas Cowboys nine-year, US$85.5 million contract with Troy Aikman (1999–2007); and in hockey Pittsburgh inked a seven-year, US$48 million pact with Jaromir Jagr (1998–2004). The next highest salary packages in hockey are: Pavel Bure's US$47-million deal over six years with Florida; Mike Modano's six-year, US$43.5-million agreement with Dallas (1998–2003); and the ill-fated deferred payment deal between Mario Lemieux and Pittsburgh for US$42 million between 1992–1997. None of the contracts included possible performance bonuses.

6.9   B.   US$3.6 million

Trying to get a new contract by refusing to play in 1999–2000 might have worked in any American city but not in small-market Ottawa and not with Senators owner Rod Bryden, whose steadfast refusal to renegotiate cost Alexei Yashin and his agent Mark Gandler US$3.6 million. Yashin, on the advice of Gandler who completely misjudged Bryden's resolve, spent the season working out with Switzerland's Kloten Flyers in hopes that his Ottawa contract would expire. But an independent arbitrator ruled in favour of the Senators and Yashin's loss seemed even greater. Had he played in 1999–2000, the $3.6 million would be in the bank and he could have negotiated his "dream" contract in 2000–01, at a potential of US$6 to $8 million a year. Instead Yashin was forced to play for $3.6 million in 2000–01 and his future market value remained in doubt. As a further insult, when Yashin took the arbitrator's decision to court to have the ruling overturned, he lost his union's (the NHLPA) backing and ultimately his right to restricted free agency. Further, he was ordered to pay the NHL's one-day legal fees of $27,649.39.

6.10 C. A 153 per cent increase
He was the goalie nobody wanted. Playing for the Canadian national team program, Fred Brathwaite caught fire in Calgary after a rash of injuries left the Flames with few options in 1999–2000. Brathwaite stayed for a team-high 61 games that season, earning a 25–25–7 record and a salary of US$ 375,000 as one of the league's lowest-paid goalies. At the six-hour arbitration hearing, Brathwaite was looking to triple his annual salary to more than US$1 million, while Calgary's qualifying offer included a standard 10 per cent raise. The decision: the Flames were ordered to pay Brathwaite US$950,000 in 2000–01 and US$1.05 million in 2001–02, a 153 and 180 per cent increase in the first and second years.

6.11 A. Philadelphia's John LeClair
John LeClair, who had scored the most total goals (235) over the preceding five years of any NHLer, had been underpaid for years by the Philadelphia Flyers. In August 2000, LeClair won a record-setting one-year arbitration award of US$7 million, beating the previous high set by Pierre Turgeon at US$4.6 million. And LeClair didn't get what he wanted. He asked for US$9 million, while the Flyers countered with US$4.6 million. Still, his pay hike from US$3.7 million in 1999–2000 to US$7 million was a 90 per cent salary raise.

6.12 D. US$20 million
After six concussions and earnings of about US$47.5 million since 1992, Eric Lindros found himself teamless in 2000–01. Lindros, once hockey's most sought after players who had twice refused early-career team offers (Sault St. Marie, Quebec), was now in limbo, a victim of the merciless waiting game imposed by Philadelphia general manager Bob Clarke and a market limited to a few teams that could afford both his salary and the quality players to trade. If an injury limited him to fewer than 20 games in 2000–01, Lindros received full payment on a US$20 million personal insurance policy.

6.13 D. 1,215 cards
According to the *Financial Post* in December 2000 there were 1,215 Wayne Gretzky cards being auctioned on eBay's web site. The highest asking price for Gretzky's 1979 rookie card was listed at US$908; the Great One's lowest was one cent.

6.14 B. US$600,000
The Sedin twins inked identical contracts when they signed with Vancouver in 1999. In 2000–01 they each earned a maximum base salary of US$1.025 million, not including $600,000 in bonus money if they won the Calder Trophy as best rookie. They would get $500,000 for coming second, $400,000 for coming third and so on. The Sedins were also eligible to earn bonuses for 20 or more goals ($300,000), 35 or more assists ($300,000), 60 or more points ($300,000), .73 points per game/minimum of 42 games ($300,000) and a plus-10 or better with the Canucks qualifying for the playoffs ($300,000). In years two and three of the Sedins' contract, the brothers could receive bonus payouts for ice time, major trophies and all-star votes.

6.15 A. Jean Beliveau
Salary disclosure was almost unheard of during the six-team era, but when Jean Beliveau signed with Montreal in October 1953 the deal was so huge that it was impossible to keep from the media when it was announced. Beliveau received $110,000 with a five-year guarantee and a slew of bonuses. He immediately became the league's highest paid athlete, making more money than the league's best players, Maurice Richard and Gordie Howe. Many believe that Beliveau was even making more money than Howe and Richard when he was playing minor pro hockey with the Quebec Aces of the Quebec Senior Hockey League. If so, Beliveau is the only minor pro star ever able to make such a claim.

6.16 B. US$243,750

Among the 737 NHLers drawing salaries at the start of 2000–01, only eight earned less than US$300,000. The lowest paid players were Vancouver's Matt Cooke, a fourth-line winger who kills penalties, and Ottawa's Karel Rachunek, a first-year defenseman from the Czech Republic. Each drew US$243,750 in 2000–01.

6.17 D. More than US$1 billion

At the start of the 2000–01 season NHL teams doled out a combined payroll of exactly US$1,001,999,328 to 737 players. It was the first time in its 83-year history that league player salaries topped the $1-billion mark. The total did not include frontline unsigned free agents such as Eric Lindros, Scott Niedermayer, Jozef Stumpel or Jason Arnott, all of whom would drive the salary average even higher once they get deals. Although the escalation is due in part to two new expansion teams, in Columbus and Minnesota, the biggest expense is player costs. In 2000–01, 16 players earned US$7 million or more; 32 players made US$5 million or more; and 46 players received US$4 million or more. The top salary earners were Anaheim's Paul Kariya and Colorado's Peter Forsberg who break the bank at US$10 million each.

6.18 B. US$148 million

According to *Forbes* magazine the average value of an NHL team was US$148 million in 2000–01, the figures ranging from US$263 million for the New York Rangers to the Edmonton Oilers at US$77 million. Franchises increased their value by an average of 10 per cent over the previous season through sponsorship revenues at new arenas. The Los Angeles Kings had the largest percentage increase, up 47 percent to US$160 million for 11th place overall. The Kings signed 10 lucrative corporate sponsorship deals paying up to $3 million a year each. As a comparison the New York Knicks topped the NBA list at US$395 million. (Expansion clubs were excluded from the list.)

6.19 D. The Toronto Maple Leafs

Figures released by Team Marketing Report of Chicago, show that the highest average ticket price for an NHL game in 2000–01 was in Toronto at $67.01, followed by New York ($65.82), Colorado ($63.11), Philadelphia ($62.31) and Dallas ($56.43). The five least costliest averages were: Calgary ($32.86), New York Islanders ($34.68), Edmonton ($34.85), Montreal ($38.36) and Washington ($38.42) Ticket prices increased over the previous year 4.3 per cent due to the opening of several new arenas. After leading for four straight years as the priciest pro team sport in North America, hockey fell to third behind the NBA ($51.02) and the NFL ($48.97) but ahead of Major League Baseball ($16.65). The Chicago-based newsletter also tabulated the cost of a family of four to attend a game. The NHL average purchase price of four tickets, four soft-drinks, two beer, four hot dogs, two hats, two programs and parking totalled $264.77.

Game 6

THE LAST ORIGINAL SIX SURVIVOR

Who was the last Original Six player (pre-1967) to play in the NHL? Unscramble the old-timers' names below by placing each letter in the correct order in the boxes. Each name starts with the bolded letter. Unscramble the letters in the circled and diamond-shaped boxes. The circled boxes spell our secret Original Six survivor and the diamond-shaped boxes, the team he played with his entire 17-year career. The letters in the darkened circles are his initials; while the letter in the darkened triangle is the initial of his team's name.

(Solutions are on page 121)

O E W **H**

CAD **R** R I H

T A K I **M** I

C U Y **B** K

SONR **A** GRTM

M N O S H

L A M **U** N L

of

92

7
BENCH WIZARDS

When Scotty Bowman coached Detroit's first game of the new millennium on January 2, 2000, it marked another major accomplishment for hockey's winningest coach. The game, a 4–3 loss to Pittsburgh, commemorated the first time that one man coached in five decades of NHL hockey. In this chapter we honour the winnings of Bowman and his colleagues behind the bench, both in regular-season play and on the trail to the Stanley Cup.

(Answers are on page 97)

7.1 Which NHL team hired the first European-trained head coach in league history?
A. The Pittsburgh Penguins
B. The Detroit Red Wings
C. The Washington Capitals
D. The Chicago Blackhawks

7.2 As of 2000–01, which individual from the four major pro sports leagues in North America has coached the most games?
A. The NHL's Scotty Bowman
B. MLB's Connie Mack
C. The NBA's Lenny Wilkens
D. The NFL's George Halas

7.3 What team has captured the most Stanley Cups with rookie head coaches?
A. The Toronto Maple Leafs
B. The Detroit Red Wings
C. The old Ottawa Senators
D. The Montreal Canadiens

7.4 Name the only NHL coach who began his career as bench boss to two Canadian junior teams, one owned by Wayne Gretzky and the other by Patrick Roy?
A. Pat Burns
B. Dave King
C. Alain Vigneault
D. Joel Quenneville

7.5 What is the highest number of goals scored in a come-from-behind win in NHL history?
A. Four goals
B. Five goals
C. Six goals
D. Seven goals

7.6 What is the fewest number of regular-season games worked in a year by an NHL head coach who then went on to lead his team to the Stanley Cup?
A. Fewer than 10 games
B. Between 10 and 44 games
C. Between 44 and 70 games
D. More than 70 games

7.7 Who was Patrick Roy's coach when he got his first NHL victory?
A. Pat Burns
B. Jacques Demers
C. Jean Perron
D. Jacques Lemaire

7.8 Who is the winningest general manager in NHL history?
A. Atlanta/Calgary/Toronto's Cliff Fletcher
B. Edmonton/New York's Glen Sather
C. The New York Islanders' Bill Torrey
D. Boston's Harry Sinden

7.9 What is the most number of Original Six teams coached in one career?
A. Two Original Six teams
B. Three Original Six teams
C. Four Original Six teams
D. Five Original Six teams

7.10 What is the most number of NHL teams for which a head coach has worked before winning a Stanley Cup?
A. Three teams
B. Four teams
C. Five teams
D. Six teams

7.11 Which NHL bench boss coached one team the longest without winning the Stanley Cup?
A. Chicago's Billy Reay
B. Boston's Milt Schmidt
C. Detroit's Sid Abel
D. Washington's Brian Murray

7.12 Who drafted the first international player in NHL history?
A. Scotty Bowman
B. Freddy Shero
C. Punch Imlach
D. Bill Torrey

7.13 Head coaches sometimes labour years with one team before capturing a Stanley Cup with that team. What is the greatest number of games worked with one team by a head coach who went on to win the Cup with that club?
A. Fewer than 300 games
B. Between 300 and 400 games
C. Between 400 and 500 games
D. More than 500 games

7.14 Which NHL head coach set a league record for his 2,000th game in 2000–01.
A. Mike Keenan
B. Scotty Bowman
C. Roger Neilson
D. Ken Hitchcock

7.15 Including New Jersey's Larry Robinson in 1999–2000, how many coaches have won the Stanley Cup after taking over their team at some point during the regular season?
A. Only one, Larry Robinson
B. Two coaches
C. Three coaches
D. Six coaches

7.16 What is the most number of new coaches hired at the start of a season?
A. Four coaches
B. Six coaches
C. Eight coaches
D. 10 coaches

7.17 How many NHL coaches once played for NHL teams coached by Scotty Bowman?
A. Fewer than 10 coaches
B. Between 10 and 20 coaches
C. Between 20 and 30 coaches
D. More than 30 coaches

7.18 As of 2000–01, which coach has recorded the most regular-season wins without winning the Stanley Cup?
A. Bryan Murray
B. Pat Quinn
C. Billy Reay
D. Roger Neilson

BENCH WIZARDS
Answers

7.1 **D. The Chicago Blackhawks**
After signing a three-year contract in February 2000 as assistant coach with Pittsburgh, Ivan Hlinka looked to be the replacement for the Penguins' Herb Brooks and the first born-and-bred European head coach in the NHL. But Chicago director of hockey operations Mike Smith, no stranger to international hockey, hired Finnish native Alpo Suhonen in April 2000, just prior to Hlinka's appointment in Pittsburgh in June of that year. The hiring of two European-trained coaches after 82 years of NHL play (Russian-born Johnny Gottselig coached Chicago in the mid-1940s but was raised in Winnipeg) was long overdue and signaled a new era in the league's head coaching fraternity. Much like the arrival of European players, Euro bench bosses were "breaking new ground," according to Columbus coach Dave King, ex-coach of Canada's national team. Why did it take so long to hire Europeans? Good question. Suhonen coached more than 1,500 games in Europe and 300 as an assistant coach in the NHL; Hlinka, coach of the 1998 Czech Olympic gold-medal team, is credited with building his country's ice hockey program into one of the world's best programs.

7.2 **B. MLB's Connie Mack**
Disparity between schedule lengths (number of games played per season) gives baseball managers a clear advantage in this category in any statistical comparison of North America's four major team sports. While no other individual in hockey comes close to Scotty Bowman's remarkable 2,000 career games-coached mark of November 24, 2000, Connie Mack (1894–1950) leads baseball with 7,755 games managed, Lenny Wilkens (1969–2000) tops basketball with 2,171 games and George Halas (1928–1968) heads football with 497 games.

7.3 **D. The Montreal Canadiens**

The Montreal Canadiens captured an unprecedented four of their record 24 Stanley Cups with rookie coaches, each Cup in successive decades between the 1950s and 1980s. The great Toe Blake coached just 70 games in the NHL before winning the Cup in 1955–56. Claude Ruel won 1968–69's championship after 76 games with the Habs; rookie Al MacNeil replaced Ruel with 55 games remaining in 1970–71 and won the Cup; and Jean Perron became Montreal's fourth Cup-winning rookie head coach after coaching 80 games in 1985–86. As of 2000–01, only 12 head coaches won the Stanley Cup in their first NHL year.

7.4 **C. Alain Vigneault**

The Montreal Canadiens ex-head coach's resume includes eight seasons coaching in the Quebec Major Junior Hockey League, five seasons behind the bench with the Hull Olympics, the QMJHL club once owned by Wayne Gretzky and where Vigneault was named CHL coach of the year in 1987–88. He also coached the Beauport Harfangs (now the Quebec Ramparts) while Roy was one of the owners. It was Vigneault's last stop in junior hockey before joining the Canadiens in 1997–98. As an NHLer, Vigneault played parts of two seasons after being drafted by St. Louis in the 1981 NHL Entry Draft.

7.5 **C. Six goals**

The difference was a measly one second but it was enough for St. Louis to stage the greatest comeback in NHL history. On November 29, 2000, the Blues scored six straight goals against Toronto in 15 minutes and 27 seconds, just one second faster than the previous mark held by Chicago in their league-record 15:28 comeback after a 5–0 deficit against Toronto on January 26, 1987. St. Louis's upset began on a third-period goalie change by coach Joel Quenneville, who pulled Roman Turek in favour of Brent Johnson. Two minutes later at 4:51 Pronger got the first of six straight St. Louis goals as the Blues won on a

Jochen Hecht goal at 18 seconds in overtime. During the come-back the Blues leading scorer Pierre Turgeon was benched and played only four minutes 18 seconds in the third period. After the St. Louis comeback one member of the Blues offered: "It felt great. They're (Toronto) the most arrogant team in the league. All they do is yap. This will shut them up."

7.6   A.   Fewer than 10 games
A dozen NHL coaches have led their teams to the Stanley Cup in their first season behind the bench, but the leader in this category is not a rookie coach. New Jersey's Larry Robinson worked four years (328 games) in Los Angeles before returning to the Devils as an assistant coach in 1999–2000. (Robinson first tenured as a Devil assistant coach under Jacques Lemaire.) With just eight games remaining in the season New Jersey general manager Lou Lamoriello fired head coach Robbie Ftorek and moved Robinson into the hot seat, where he gelled the underachieving Devils into Stanley Cup winners. The Devils went just 4–4–0 before the playoffs, but under Robinson they dismissed Florida in four games, Toronto in six, Philadelphia in seven and Dallas in six, including an extraordinary triple-overtime loss in game five and a double-overtime Cup clincher in game six. New Jersey became the first team in two decades (since the 1980 Islanders) to whip three 100-point teams en route to the Cup. No NHL head coach has ever coached so few regular-season games with a team that went on to win the Stanley Cup. Ironically, just a year earlier, after a miserable final season in Los Angeles, Robinson was asked whether he planned to return behind the bench next season. He said: "Oh yes, I love sleepless nights."

7.7   D.   Jacques Lemaire
Jacques Lemaire coached only 97 games in Montreal, the team he won eight Stanley Cups with as a player, but in one of those games Lemaire inserted 19-year old Patrick Roy in his first game. Roy, a prospect drafted 51st overall by Montreal in 1984, was

called up from Granby of the Quebec Major Junior Hockey League as a back-up against Winnipeg on February 23, 1985. To his surprise Lemaire put him in after two periods in the 4–4 game. "Jacques Lemaire came into the dressing room and he said: 'Roy, get in the net,'" Roy recalled. "My English was not very good. I turned around and I looked at Guy Carbonneau. I said: "Did he mention my name?' Carbo goes: 'Yeah, You're going in.'" Montreal won the game but Roy headed back to the minors before joining the team fulltime in 1985–86—leading the Canadiens to the Stanley Cup.

7.8   D. Boston's Harry Sinden
In 29 seasons as Boston's general manager Harry Sinden presided over six conference titles, 10 divisional championships and 1,170 wins, the most victories by a GM in league annals. Although Sinden coached the 1970 Bruins to a Stanley Cup, he has never brought home hockey's most coveted prize as a general manager. Critics and fans say Sinden is "more interested in returning a profit than returning the Cup," which the Bruins haven't won since 1972. Sinden is the only GM to notch 1,000 wins.

MOST REGULAR-SEASON WINS BY AN NHL GM

GM	Team	Years	Wins
Harry Sinden	Boston	29	1,170
Cliff Fletcher	Atl/Cal, Tor	26	942
Jack Adams	Detroit	35	913
Emile Francis	NYR, St.L, Hfd	25	841
Glen Sather	Edm, NYR	21	768
Bill Torrey	NYI	20	756

Current to 1999–2000/courtesy of The Hockey News

7.9 B. Three Original Six teams

In 1999–2000 Mike Keenan became just the third bench boss to have coached half of the Original Six teams; Dick Irvin was the first and Pat Burns the second. Irvin coached Chicago, Toronto and Montreal during a 27-year span during the 1940s and 1950s; Burns was Montreal's coach before moving to Toronto and Boston; and Keenan split coaching duties with Chicago, New York and Boston.

7.10 B. Four teams

No NHL coach has been behind the bench with as many teams before winning the Stanley Cup as Jacques Demers, who was working on his fourth NHL team, the Montreal Canadiens, when he led them to the championship in 1992-93. Demers' bench career began in the NHL-rival WHA where he had already coached another four clubs during the 1970s, bringing his total to eight pro teams before his Cup in 1993. When the WHA joined the NHL in 1979–80 Demers coached the Quebec Nordiques for one season. After two years in the AHL with Quebec's Fredericton team, he went to St. Louis for three seasons and led the Blues to within one game of the Stanley Cup finals (losing to Calgary) in 1986. Recognized as a masterful motivator who could get the most out of a club's players, Demers spent four years in Detroit where he became the first coach in NHL history to win the Jack Adams Award as top coach two consecutive seasons. Coaches Mike Keenan and old-timer Art Ross each coached three teams before capturing hockey's highest honour.

7.11 A. Chicago's Billy Reay

Billy Reay coached some of the 1960s' and early 1970s' highest scoring teams but never a Stanley Cup winner. Chicago's coach for 14 seasons, Reay was an institution in the Blackhawk organization, leading the club to numerous West Division titles, a first-place finish overall in regular-season standings for the first time in franchise history (1966–67) and, unfortunately, to the

Cup finals an agonizing three times without sipping champagne. During the regular season he coached 1,012 games in Chicago, more matches with one team than any other Cup-less coach in league history; but he also won more (542 games) than any other bench boss of his era, except Dick Irvin. No other coach challenges Reay's games coached numbers, either on one team or in a career, but the Murray Brothers (Bryan and Terry) combined to record 997 games coached in Washington between 1981–82 to 1993–94 inclusive without a Cup.

MOST GAMES COACHED, ONE TEAM, BY A CUP-LESS COACH

Coach	Team	Years	GC
Billy Reay	Chicago	1963–1977	1,012
Sid Abel	Detroit	1957–1970	811
Milt Schmidt	Boston	1954–1966	726
Bryan Murray	Washington	1981–1990	672
Emile Francis	NYR	1965–1975	654
Michel Bergeron	Quebec	1980–1989	634

Current to 2000–01

7.12   A.   Scotty Bowman

The first international player selected in an NHL draft was Finnish-born Tommi Salmalainen, who actually played hockey for HIFK Helsinki in Finland. Salmalainen was picked 66th overall by St. Louis coach/general manager Scotty Bowman in 1969. Although Salmalainen never played a game in the NHL, Bowman demonstrated an early willingness to experiment with European players who were trained in a free-flowing style of game that he employed to much success in Montreal, Buffalo, Pittsburgh and Detroit. After Bowman selected Salmalainen in 1969, five years passed before the first trickle of Europeans were selected into the NHL.

7.13 **D. More than 500 games**

The success rate of modern-day coaches largely determines their longevity behind the bench. That do-or-die philosophy was no different with New York coach Al Arbour who coached 558 games in seven consecutive winning seasons during the 1970s before the Islanders' first Stanley Cup in 1980. In NHL history no bench boss's career has survived as many games before a Stanley Cup victory. If the record were based on seasons coached instead of games coached, this distinction would fall to Boston's legendary Art Ross, who was behind the bench for 12 seasons (530 games) before the Bruins' Cup win in 1938–39. Detroit's renowned Jack Adams coached 416 games and nine seasons before his Red Wings won their first championship in 1935–36.

7.14 **B. Scotty Bowman**

Even though Scotty Bowman played down his feat, saying: "It's not a big deal...you don't count games," it was a memorable milestone for hockey's longest-serving bench boss. Bowman earned his 2,000th game with a Detroit 3–2 victory against Vancouver on November 24, 2000, almost 33 years to the day after his first game on November 22, 1967. The win, before a sold-out crowd at Joe Louis Arena, came on a late goal by Sergei Fedorov, who wasn't even born when Bowman took his first job behind an NHL bench. (Fedorov was born two years after Bowman debuted with St. Louis in 1967.) Or put it another way: Vince Lombardi was still coaching the Green Bay Packers when Bowman was with the Blues. His longevity can be attributed to his ability to succeed through changing times. "He's an old-school guy who's adjusted to new-school personalities," said Dallas coach Ken Hitchcock. Scotty's 2,000-game mark had a win-loss-tie record of 1,157–548–295.

7.15 **C. Three coaches**

Prior to the New Jersey Devils' stunning coaching change in 1999–2000 when Larry Robinson took over from Robbie Ftorek with just eight regular-season games remaining and captured the Stanley Cup, only two other Cup-winning coaches were mid-season replacements. Dick Irvin Sr. took over for Art Duncan to win Toronto's Stanley Cup in 1931–32 and Claude Ruel was bounced in favour of Al MacNeil during 1970–71 when Montreal won the championship.

7.16 D. 10 coaches

Of the NHL's 28 franchises in the league in 1997–98, 10 clubs hired new coaches for the start of the season. The 10 new coaches were: Alain Vigneault (Montreal), Darryl Sutter (San Jose), Lindy Ruff (Buffalo), Ron Wilson (Washington), Pierre Page (Anaheim), Jim Schoenfeld (Phoenix), Kevin Constantine (Pittsburgh), Brian Sutter (Calgary), Pat Burns (Boston) and Wayne Cashman (Philadelphia). Only three—Ruff, Sutter and Wilson—survived more than three seasons into December 2000.

7.17 C. Between 20 and 30 coaches

No one has had more influence on NHL coaching than Scotty Bowman. The first man to coach at the NHL level for five decades, Bowman has not only influenced the likes of many coaches such as Mike Keenan, who never played under him, but, at last count, according to *The Hockey News,* 27 former Bowman players who themselves went on to coach NHL teams. Among these elite alumni as of 2000–01 are former St. Louis players: Terry Crisp, Al Arbour, Red Berenson, Jim Roberts and Barclay Plager; Montreal players: Larry Robinson, Bob Gainey, Mario Tremblay, Jacques Lemaire, Yvan Cournoyer, Steve Shutt and Jacques Laperriere; and Buffalo players: Craig Ramsay, Jim Schoenfeld, Rick Dudley, Andre Savard and Lindy Ruff. That number is likely to increase once former Bowman players from Pittsburgh and Detroit hang up the pads for a crack behind the bench.

7.18 C. Billy Reay

No coach in NHL history has won more games in the regular season without capturing a Stanley Cup championship than Billy Reay of Chicago. Reay, fourth in all-time wins among all NHL coaches with 542 victories, played bridesmaid three times in the Cup finals.

MOST WINS BY A CUP-LESS COACH

Coach	Teams	Years	GC	Wins
Billy Reay	Tor, Chi	1957–1977	1,102	542
Bryan Murray	Was, Det, Fla	1981–1998	975	484
Roger Neilson	Tor, Buf, Van, LA, NYR, Fla, Phi	1977–2000	998	459
Pat Quinn	Phi, LA, Van, Tor	1978–2000	908	447
Pat Burns	Mon, Tor, Bos	1988–2000	847	409

Current to 1999–2000

Game 7

SILVERWARE STARS

Each year the NHL awards more than a dozen individuals trophies for on-ice performance and outstanding contributions away from the rink. In this game match the 10 trophies awarded during the 1990s in the left column and the player who received them in the right.

(Solutions are on page 121)

1. _____ 1990 Hart Trophy (Regular-season MVP)

    A. Mario Lemieux

2. _____ 1991 Calder Trophy (Rookie of the year)

    B. Dominik Hasek

3. _____ 1992 Art Ross Trophy (Leading scorer)

    C. Cam Neely

4. _____ 1993 Frank Selke Trophy (Defensive forward)

    D. Paul Kariya

5. _____ 1994 Bill Masterton Trophy (Dedication to hockey)

    E. Mark Messier

6. _____ 1995 Vezina Trophy (Best goalie)

    F. Doug Gilmour

7. _____ 1996 Conn Smythe Trophy (Playoff MVP)

    G. Rob Blake

8. _____ 1997 Lady Byng Trophy (Sportsmanship)

    H. Teemu Selanne

9. _____ 1998 Norris Trophy (Best defenseman)

    I. Joe Sakic

10. _____ 1999 M. Richard Trophy (Most goals)

    J. Ed Belfour

8
THE SHOWDOWN

What do Buffalo fans have to do to get some respect? The hometown Bills couldn't win a Super Bowl in four consecutive trips to the big game, then drop a 1999 playoff opener to Tennessee on a heart-wrenching last-second kick return, and, in hockey, the Sabres lose the 1999 Stanley Cup on Brett Hull's controversial foot-in-the-crease Cup-winner. Then came a demon of another kind, a phantom goal that sank the Sabres in a 2–1 loss to Philadelphia in game two of 2000's opening playoff round. Trailing 1–0, John LeClair's shot entered the net through a hole in the mesh. No video replay picked up the problem and play continued until a Sportsnet net camera showed the puck going in *outside* of the post. By then, under NHL rules, it was too late. Hey, anything can happen at the show.

(*Answers are on page 112*)

8.1 How many liquid ounces does the bowl of the Stanley Cup hold?
   A. 50 ounces
   B. 100 ounces
   C. 200 ounces
   D. 300 ounces

8.2 How many Devils won Stanley Cups with both of New Jersey's championship teams from 1994–95 and 1999–2000?
   A. Six players
   B. Nine players
   C. 12 players
   D. 15 players

8.3 How many NHL seasons did Mario Lemieux play before he experienced his first playoff game?

    A. Two seasons

    B. Three seasons

    C. Four seasons

    D. Five seasons

8.4 After losing the 1999 Stanley Cup to Dallas on Brett Hull's disputed goal, how long did it take the Buffalo Sabres to get their first victory in 1999–2000?

    A. The Sabres won the first game of 1999–2000

    B. Three games

    C. Five games

    D. Seven games

8.5 As of the 2000 postseason, who played in the most playoff games without winning the Stanley Cup?

    A. Dale Hunter

    B. Brad Park

    C. Ray Bourque

    D. Brian Propp

8.6 What was Detroit's regular-season point difference between 1995–96, the year they recorded a league-high 62 regular-season wins, and 1996–97, the year they won the Stanley Cup?

    A. Less than 15 points

    B. 15 to 25 points

    C. 25 to 35 points

    D. More than 35 points

8.7 Who was the Dallas crowd taunting when they chanted "Eddie's better" during the 2000 Stanley Cup Western Conference finals?

    A. Patrick Roy

    B. Curtis Joseph

C. Martin Brodeur

D. Ron Tugnutt

8.8 Who was the first Russian-trained player to score a goal in a Stanley Cup final?

A. Igor Kravchuk of the Chicago Blackhawks

B. Alexei Kovalev of the New York Rangers

C. Alexei Zhitnik of the Los Angeles Kings

D. Pavel Bure of the Vancouver Canucks

8.9 Which team iced the first Swedish-trained players to appear in the Stanley Cup finals?

A. The Detroit Red Wings

B. The Calgary Flames

C. The New York Rangers

D. The Toronto Maple Leafs

8.10 Defenseman Michel Petit shares the NHL record for playing with 10 NHL teams, but what is the record for most teams by a player who won the Stanley Cup?

A. Four teams

B. Six teams

C. Eight teams

D. 10 teams

8.11 Besides the Stanley Cup champion New Jersey Devils in 1999–2000, how many other NHL clubs have defeated three 100-point teams en route to the championship?

A. None

B. Only one other team

C. Three teams

D. Five teams

8.12 Who leads the NHL in career penalty minutes in the playoffs?

A. Dale Hunter

B. Dave Williams

C. Chris Nilan

D. Claude Lemieux

8.13 In 18 NHL seasons, defenseman and supreme shot-blocker Craig Ludwig scored just 38 goals. How many playoff goals did he amass during his career between 1982–83 and 1999–2000?

A. None

B. Four goals

C. Eight goals

D. 16 goals

8.14 When the New Jersey Devils won the Stanley Cup in 1995, they broke a record for the most Americans on a Stanley Cup winner that dates back to which season?

A. 1937–38

B. 1957–58

C. 1977–78

D. 1987–88

8.15 During the NHL's six-team era from 1942–43 to 1966–67, what is the highest number of points a team finished out of first place in the regular season and went on to win the Stanley Cup?

A. Fewer than 15 points

B. Between 15 and 20 points

C. Between 20 and 25 points

D. More than 25 points

8.16 Which Stanley Cup-winning team finished the regular season with the highest number of points out of first place since NHL expansion in 1967?

A. The Montreal Canadiens of 1970-71
B. The New York Islanders of 1979-80
C. The Montreal Canadiens of 1985-86
D. The Colorado Avalanche of 1995-96

8.17 In what year did the first Finnish-trained player score a goal in the Stanley Cup finals?

A. 1965
B. 1975
C. 1985
D. 1995

8.18 What modern-day goalie holds the NHL record for most career shutouts in the playoffs?

A. Jacques Plante
B. Ken Dryden
C. Grant Fuhr
D. Patrick Roy

8.19 Montreal's Henri Richard played on a record 11 Stanley Cup winners during his illustrious career. How many championship rings does he still have in his possession?

A. None
B. Only one ring
C. Five rings
D. All 11 rings

THE SHOWDOWN
Answers

8.1   B.   100 ounces
According to the Hockey Hall of Fame, guardians of hockey's most cherished trophy, the Stanley Cup bowl holds 100 liquid ounces or about four 750 ml bottles of champagne.

8.2   B.   Nine players
New Jersey general manager Lou Lamoriello's sixth sense for team building is the main reason the Devils captured a couple of Stanley Cups between 1995 and 2000. Give credit to the intimidating play of Scott Stevens, the return to form of Martin Brodeur and the inspired coaching of Larry Robinson, but it was Lamoriello who built the Devils around a core of character and role players designed to win over the long haul. And he kept them together, even in an ice age when player mobility is a given among managers. (How many teams have more than a half-dozen players still in the fold six years later?) Robinson, assistant coach Bobby Carpenter and nine players—Scott Stevens, Martin Brodeur, Sergei Brylin, Ken Daneyko, Bobby Holik, Claude Lemieux, Randy McKay, Scott Niedermayer and Chris Terreri—won two Cups with the Devils. Only pesky Claude Lemieux left during the intervening years between championships.

8.3   D.   Five seasons
Mario Lemieux's first career playoff game was a 3–1 win over the New York Rangers on April 5, 1989. He had played five NHL seasons or 368 games without a whiff of postseason action. By the time the Penguins seriously challenged for the Stanley Cup in 1991, Lemieux had just 11 playoff games under his belt in seven NHL seasons. A two-time Cup champion before his first retirement in 1997, Lemieux played in just 89 playoff games.

8.4   D. Seven games

After losing the 1999 Stanley Cup on Brett Hull's controversial toe-in-the-crease goal, the Sabres went winless in their first seven games (0–5–2) in 1999–2000. The season-opening slump equalled their worst start in franchise history (0–4–3 in 1990–91). "Our attitudes aren't great right now. There's too many guys just showing up," said Sabres captain Mike Peca. Buffalo winger Dixon Ward joked: "Until we get an apology we're not going to win a game. We vow not to win until we get an apology from (NHL commissioner Gary) Bettman." The Sabres got none; and had to walk away from a regular season where the NHL reviewed 289 goals on video and disallowed 137, most for a toe in the crease. Hull's Cup-winner was a bitter pill for Buffalo, who were down 3–2 against Dallas in the series. Their first win of the following season, 1999–2000, came in a 7–3 victory over Carolina on October 22. It was Buffalo's eighth game of the season.

8.5   C. Ray Bourque

As of the 2000 playoffs, no NHLer had seen more postseason time without hoisting the Stanley Cup than Ray Bourque. Bourque, who remained Cup-less through 21 seasons, had amassed 193 games—more than two complete regular seasons of playoff action. He came closest twice in 1988 and 1990 when the Bruins met the Edmonton Oilers in the Cup finals, both times in losing causes. Only Dale Hunter's 186-game playoff run rivals Bourque's fruitless quest. Hunter's best chance at a Cup came in 1998 when Washington met Detroit in the finals. But the Red Wings had the brooms out and swept the Capitals four straight. Both Bourque and Hunter got second chances at a Cup after being traded, courtesy of their respective clubs, to the Cup-contending Colorado Avalanche. In both cases, Hunter in 1999 and Bourque in 2000, the Avs bailed in the third round against Dallas. Hunter's hopes for a Cup were over (he retired in 1999), but Bourque played on with Colorado in 2000–01. Brad Park and Brian Propp played 161 and 160 playoff games without earning a championship.

8.6   **D. More than 35 points**

A big regular season guarantees nothing but home ice advantage in the playoffs. Detroit found that out in 1995–96 after establishing the best wins and points in NHL history with a 62–13–7 record. They finished the season 27 points ahead of second-place Colorado but lost their playoff bid in the third round to the Avalanche. The following season, 1996–97, Detroit wised up and saved something for the playoffs, finishing with twice as many regular-season losses over the previous year and 13 points back of first-place. The strategy worked. With just 94 points in 1996–97 Detroit finished 37 points behind 1995–96's mark of 131, but the Red Wings went on to win their first Stanley Cup since 1955.

8.7   **A. Patrick Roy**

The 2000 Western Conference finals between heavyweights Dallas and Colorado featured hockey's two premier goaltenders in a classic showdown of battling egos: Patrick Roy against Ed Belfour. In the winner-take-all seventh game for the West's Stanley Cup finalist, Belfour and Roy duelled through 60 minutes to a 2–2 deadlock. During the match Dallas fans began chanting "E-dd-ie's better, E-dd-ie's better," jeering at Roy, often regarded as the game's best money goalie. Then, at 12:10 in sudden-death overtime, Joe Nieuwendyk scored the series winner, sending the fans into pandemonium and Roy to the links to lick his wounds.

8.8   **B. Alexei Kovalev of the New York Rangers**

The NHL record book notes than Alexei Kovalev was the first Russian to score a Stanley Cup finals goal, but there's no mention of how close Pavel Bure came to beating him and being first. Kovalev scored at 8:29 of the third period of game one of the 1994 Rangers-Canucks finals. Bure, the second Russian to notch a Cup final goal, potted his goal just a little more than a game later, at 1:03 of the first period in game three. Although Igor Kravchuk was the first former Soviet player to appear in a Cup final game with Chicago in 1992, he did not score. Alexei Zhitnik of the Kings was the first ex-Soviet to post a point in the finals, an assist on a Luc Robitaille goal in the 1993 Cup showdown.

8.9   C. The New York Rangers
The first Swedes to skate in a Stanley Cup final were Anders Hedberg and Ulf Nilsson of the Rangers. New York plucked the pair from the WHA Winnipeg Jets, where they starred with Bobby Hull for four seasons before their free agent signings in June 1978. The Swedes brought the Rangers style and skill; and a chance, after a seven-year absence, at the Stanley Cup in 1979. Unfortunately, New York, who had surprised everyone in the semifinals by beating the up-and-coming Islanders, met the powerhouse Montreal Canadiens. The Rangers took game one but never won another match. Hedberg scored one goal in the Cup finals, a NHL first for a Swede, while Nilsson appeared in just two games.

8.10   D. 10 teams
In 2000–01 Michel Petit's 10-team league record was equaled by childhood friend J.J. Daigneault, who played on his tenth team, the Minnesota Wild, January 12, 2001. "It has been a great ride," Daigneault, 35, said in a *National Post* story. "It has been a lot of fun. When I played for four or five teams, it was not a big deal. But now 10 teams . . . wow." It was Daigneault's 898th career game after stops with Vancouver, Philadelphia, Montreal, St. Louis, Pittsburgh, Anaheim, the New York Islanders, Nashville and Phoenix. The hardest team to leave was his beloved Canadiens, where he played the longest, six seasons, and won a Stanley Cup in 1993. "We'll see what the future holds. I'd like to play in Europe. I know I have never played there."

8.11   B. Only one other team
As of 2000–01, only two Stanley Cup champions have battled three 100-point regular-season teams during their playoff drive. In 1979–80 the 91-point New York Islanders won their first

Stanley Cup after defeating three of the top four regular-season teams in their four playoff series. The Isles beat Los Angeles (74 points), Boston (105 points), Buffalo (110 points) and Philadelphia (116 points). It was an NHL first. New Jersey's championship in 2000 was just the second time three 100-point teams lost to the Stanley Cup winners. The Devils overcame Florida (98 points), Toronto (100 points), Philadelphia (105 points) and Dallas (102 points). The extra point for overtime regular-season losses accounted for some of the Leafs, Flyers and Stars' team points. In fact, during 1999-2000 a record-tying seven NHL clubs recorded 100-points or more. In 1980, when the Islanders defeated three 100-point teams, four teams in regular-season action had 100 points or more.

8.12 A. Dale Hunter

Hunter gave his all to hockey, but unfortunately the game wasn't so kind come playoff time. His 186-game Cup-less career is second in postseason games only to Ray Bourque's pursuit of a championship. However, Hunter does find his name in the playoff records as penalty leader with a league-high 729 playoff penalty minutes, better than Chris Nilan (541), Claude Lemieux (489 and counting) and Tiger Williams (455).

8.13 B. Four goals

As one reporter observed, "It's not something you see everyday." The phenomenon happened on Thursday June 10, 1999, when Dallas old-timer Craig Ludwig scored just his fourth playoff goal in his 173rd postseason match. "Wasn't that amazing?" said teammate Mike Keane. "He's playing like he's 36 again." Later, someone asked the 38-year-old Ludwig, "When was your last playoff goal?" Ludwig deadpanned: "It was just a few minutes ago, didn't you see it." Ludwig had last scored with Montreal during the 1987–88 playoffs, 11 years earlier.

8.14 A. 1937–38

It's hard to imagine a Stanley Cup winner today without a small contingent of Americans, but 60 years ago, when the NHL was almost completely populated by Canadian players, it would be unthinkable. In the old eight-team NHL, U.S.-born players were a rarity. So when Chicago Blackhawk owner Major Fredric McLaughlin seized upon the idea of an all-American team in 1937–38, it must have been thought of as lunacy. The patriotic Major even appointed an American, major-league baseball umpire Bill Stewart, as coach. McLaughlin's boys didn't disappoint the skeptics during the regular season, as Chicago posted a sub-.500 with a 14–25–9 record. But something unexpected happened in the playoffs. His name was Mike Karakas. The Chicago netminder from Aurora, Minnesota, stole the Cup in what is still regarded as one of hockey's greatest postseason upsets. In all, a record eight Americans suited up for the Hawks during that remarkable postseason, just four fewer than the 12 who helped New Jersey to the championship in 1995.

8.15 D. More than 25 points

While the NHL reeled from Maurice Richard's stunning 50-goal season in 1944–45, the next shocker came during the playoffs courtesy of the third-place Toronto. In the first round the spunky Maple Leafs defeated Richard's first-place Canadiens in six grueling games and then pulled out a seven-game squeaker against Detroit to win the Stanley Cup. Toronto won the biggest upset of the six-team era, finishing the regular season with 52 points, 28 points behind league-leading Montreal (80 points). Interestingly, two other Toronto teams recorded the next biggest upsets between 1942–43 and 1966–67. The 1948–49 Maple Leafs finished in fourth place and 18 points back of top spot to capture the Cup; and in 1966–67, Toronto's so-called over-the-hill gang surprised Montreal with a Stanley Cup championship after finishing 19 points out of first place.

8.16 C. The Montreal Canadiens of 1985–86

During 1985–86 six teams finished ahead of Montreal in the overall standings. Edmonton, with 119 points, held an astounding 32-point spread over the Canadiens who struggled through the season to finish with 87 points. By chance during Montreal's four playoff rounds they faced only one club with a better regular-season record, the low-ranking sixth-place Calgary Flames. That and a record number of Montreal rookies, including a new goaltender by the name of Patrick Roy, made history in the finals as Montreal defeated the Flames in five games to capture their 23rd Stanley Cup title. Twenty-year-old Roy became the youngest player to win the Conn Smythe Trophy as playoff MVP.

LARGEST POINT SPREAD BETWEEN FIRST-PLACE TEAMS & CUP WINNERS*

Year	First-Place Team	Points	Stanley Cup Winner	Points	Point-Spread
1985-86	Edmonton	119	Montreal	87	32
1995-96	Detroit	131	Colorado	104	27
1979-80	Philadelphia	116	NYI	91	25
1970-71	Boston	121	Montreal	97	24
1990-91	Chicago	106	Pittsburgh	88	18
1991-92	NYR	105	Pittsburgh	87	18
1994-95	Detroit	70	New Jersey	18	18

Since 1967–68/Current to 2000

8.17 C. 1985

The first Finn to pot a Stanley Cup goal was the Flyers' Ilkka Sinisalo in 1985. Sinisalo's power play marker was the first goal of the 1985 Cup finals, coming in game one at 15:05 of the first period against Edmonton's Grant Fuhr. Sinisalo was originally signed as a free agent by Philadelphia in 1981 after a number of seasons with HIFK Helsinki in Finland. The first Finn to play in the NHL was Boston's Matti Hagman in 1977.

8.18 D. Patrick Roy

Among the many NHL goaltending records set by Patrick Roy in his twilight years is the career mark for playoff shutouts. During the 1999–2000 playoffs Roy tied Clint Benedict's amazing 73-year-old record of 15 zeroes, a mark sure to be broken by Roy during the 2001 postseason. But Roy's 196 playoff games (through 1999– 2000) dwarfs Benedict's career total of just 48, a sublime playoff performance that includes four Stanley Cups in nine playoff years with the old Ottawa Senators and Montreal Maroons. While Roy has never scored four shutouts in one play-off year, Benedict is the only netminder in NHL history to notch two postseasons of four shutouts. Jacques Plante recorded 14 shutouts in 112 playoff matches, Ken Dryden 10 in 112 games and Grant Fuhr six in 150 games.

8.19 B. Only one ring

Henri Richard won more Stanley Cups than any other NHLer, but among those 11 Cups he owns only one ring. Unfortunately, thieves stole his other championship bands from his Montreal-area home after he retired in 1975. The Canadiens great began his Hall of Fame career winning an unprecedented five consecutive Cups with Montreal between 1956 and 1960. Only one ring was issued for that dynasty, "The team paid half (the cost) of the ring and we paid half," Richard recalled in a *Montreal Gazette* story. The stolen rings were from the 1960, 1965, 1966, 1968, 1969 and 1971 seasons. His last Cup ring, 1973, is the only championship band that he still owns. The king of the rings keeps that treasure in a safe place while he wears his 1979-issued Hall of Fame ring.

SOLUTIONS

Game 1: "Stitch Me Up, Boys"

1. Don Cherry, referring to the Marty McSorley suspension: "I've got so much to say, I can't wait to hear myself say it."
2. Claude Lemieux, referring to Philadelphia's Eric Desjardins during the 2000 playoffs: "What's the "C" stand for—selfish?"
3. Patrick Roy, referring to Dominik Hasek: "I'll take my (three) rings over his (five) Vezinas."
4. Mike Milbury, after being criticized by Glen Sather about trading top ranked goalies: "They should mind their own (bleeping) business and figure out their own problems."
5. Theoren Fleury, after his first disastrous season with the Rangers: "I was

awful. Just plain awful." *The Hockey News* called it: "The worst Garden debut since Adam and Eve."
6. Maurice Richard, during the 1955 Richard Riot in Montreal: "I'm just a hockey player."
7. Jaromir Jagr, referring to his early season scoring problems after returning from Japan where the Penguins played season-openers in 2000–01: "I don't know where my hands are. Maybe I left them in Japan."
8. Steve Ludzik, Tampa Bay head coach on rookie right winger Sheldon Keefe: "He'll chew a goal post apart to put a puck in the net."

Game 2: The Shooting Gallery

Reading in descending order down the puzzle the remaining letters spell OLAF KOLZIG, Washington's South African-born goalie who won the Vezina Trophy and led the league in shots faced (1,957) and minutes played (4,371) in 1999–2000.

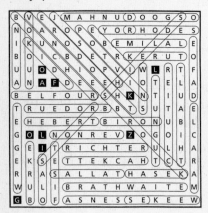

Game 3: The Euro Draftee

1. G. Tommi Salmalainen, First European draft pick, 1969. Also the first Finnish draft pick. Chosen by St. Louis 66th overall.
2. B. Per Alexandersson, First Swedish draft pick, 1974. Chosen by Toronto 49th overall.
3. F. Viktor Khatulev, First Russian draft pick, 1975. Selected 160th overall by Philadelphia.
4. A. Bjorn Johansson, First Euro drafted in the first round, 1976. Chosen fifth overall by the California Golden Seals. Johansson played only 15 games in two seasons for Cleveland.
5. D. Ladislav Svozil, First Czechoslovak draft pick, 1978. Svozil was chosen 194th overall by Detroit.
6. E. Bernhard Englbrecht, First German draft pick, 1978. Englbrecht was chosen 196th overall by Calgary.
7. C. Mats Sundin. Selected first overall by the Quebec Nordiques, 1989.

Game 4: Hockey Crossword

Game 5: The High-Fivers

1. D. Dave Andreychuk / Buffalo Sabres
2. J. Alexei Zhamnov / Winnipeg Jets
3. I. Mats Sundin / Quebec Nordiques
4. F. Joe Nieuwendyk / Calgary Flames
5. G. John Tonelli / New York Islanders
6. B. Ian Turnbull / Toronto Maple Leafs
7. K. Tim Young / Minnesota North Stars
8. C. Pat Hughes / Edmonton Oilers
9. E. Mark Pavelich / New York Rangers
10. A. Grant Mulvey / Chicago Blackhawks

Game 6: The Last Original Six Survivor

Game 7: Silverware Stars

1. E. 1990 Hart Trophy/Mark Messier
2. J. 1991 Calder Trophy/Ed Belfour
3. A. 1992 Art Ross Trophy/Mario Lemieux
4. F 1993 Frank Selke Trophy/Doug Gilmour
5. C. 1994 Bill Masterton Trophy/ Cam Neely
6. B. 1995 Vezina Trophy/ Dominik Hasek
7. I. 1996 Conn Smythe Trophy/ Joe Sakic
8. D. 1997 Lady Byng Trophy/Paul Kariya
9. G. 1998 Norris Trophy/Rob Blake
10. H. 1999 M. Richard Trophy/ Teemu Selanne

ACKNOWLEDGEMENTS

Thanks to the following publishers and organizations for the use of quoted and statistical material:

- From *The Hockey News,* various excerpts. Reprinted by permission of *The Hockey News,* a division of GTC Transcontinental Publishing, Inc.
- From The *National Post.*
- From *Total Hockey* Copyright © 1998 by Dan Diamond and Associates Inc. Published by Total Sports, 1998.
- From the *Montreal Gazette.* Published by Southam, Inc.
- From the *Globe and Mail.* Published by the Globe and Mail.
- From *The Official NHL Guide and Record Book.* Published by Total Sports Canada.

Care has been taken to trace ownership of copyright material contained in this book. The publishers welcome any information that will enable them to rectify any reference or credit in subsequent editions.

The author gratefully acknowledges the help of Steve Dryden and everyone at *The Hockey News*; Gary Meagher and Benny Ercolani of the NHL; Phil Pritchard and Craig Campbell at the Hockey Hall of Fame; the staff at the McLellan–Redpath Library at McGill University; Rob Sanders and Terri Wershler at Greystone Books; the many hockey writers, broadcast-journalists, media and Internet organizations who have made the game better through their own work; as well as editor Brian Scrivener for his dedication, expertise and humour, fact-checker Allen Bishop, Webmaster Mike Curran, graphic artist Peter van Vlaardingen and puzzle designer Adrian van Vlaardingen for their creativity. Special thanks also for the additional hockey research by Kerry Banks.